Spirit-Shaped Mission

A Holistic Charismatic Missiology

Spirit-Shaped Mission

A Holistic Charismatic Missiology

Andrew Lord

PATERNOSTER

First published in 2005 by Paternoster Press

09 08 07 06 05 04   7 6 5 4 3 2 1

Paternoster Press is an imprint of Authentic Media,
9 Holdom Avenue, Bletchley, Milton Keynes MK1 1QR, UK
and
P.O. Box 1047, Waynesboro, GA 30830-2047, USA

www.authenticmedia.co.uk

British Library Cataloguing in Publication Data
A catalogue record for this book is available from the British Library

ISBN 1-84227-264-0

Cover Design by FourNineZero
Typeset by WestKey Ltd, Falmouth, Cornwall
Print Management by Adare Carwin
Printed by J. H. Haynes & Co. Ltd., Sparkford

For Debbie, Peter, Hannah and Simeon

Contents

Studies in Pentecostal and Charismatic Issues

Consultant Editors: Max Turner, Andrew Walker
Series Editors: Mark Cartledge, Neil Hudson and Keith Warrington

Studies in Charismatic and Pentecostal Issues is a new series of academic monographs, which explore issues of interest to charismatic and Pentecostal scholars, students and leaders. The books will be multi-disciplinary covering:

- **Biblical** studies on the Spirit and spiritual gifts.
- **Historical** studies on Pentecostal-charismatic Christianity.
- Pentecostal-charismatic **theological** studies.
- **Empirical** analysis of contemporary Pentecostal-charismatic Christianity.

Acknowledgements

I would like to acknowledge the support and encouragement of a variety of people who have helped develop my thinking and practice of mission. As ever Debbie, my wife, and Peter, Hannah and Simeon, my children, have given a secure place of encouragement during the many moves and changes of recent years. Debbie's experience and insight have contributed greatly to the themes taken up in this book. My parents have always encouraged learning that has inspired me in many ways. A number of communities have shaped and challenged my thinking on mission: the Church Mission Society, with whom I served; the Centre for Missiology and World Christianity in Birmingham, with whom I first studied pentecostalism; Ridley Hall Theological College and the Faculty of Divinity in Cambridge, who stretched my theology; and the local church communities in Coventry, Leamington Spa, Lichfield, Chase Terrace, Cambridge and Milton, who challenged my practice. Thanks also to the communities in West Haddon, Long Buckby, Watford and Winwick with whom I currently serve and who have provided a warm welcome and fresh challenge in mission. Thanks to Clive Evans and Peterborough Diocese for encouraging my continued study and writing alongside local ministry. I am very thankful to Mark Cartledge for his encouragement and detailed feedback on the manuscript, to Allan Anderson for initiating many thoughts and giving opportunity to debate the thesis of this book in a research seminar, and to members of the Anglican Charismatic Theological Seminar. I am grateful for the comments of Gavin Wakefield, Brian Stanley, Peter Fulljames and Tim Dakin to earlier versions of parts of the text. Other people have provided insights that have found their way into this work in hidden ways, including Ray Simpson, Jeremy Begbie, Chris Cocksworth and Mark Ireland.

I wish to acknowledge permission for previously published material to be reproduced and adapted in this book. Permission has been gratefully received from the named publishers for the following material I have written:

To Sheffield Academic Press, Mansion House, 19 Kingfield Road, Sheffield S11 9AS, for: 'Mission Eschatology: A Framework for Mission in the Spirit', *Journal of Pentecostal Theology* 11 (1997), pp. 111–23. 'The Voluntary Principle in Pentecostal Missiology', *Journal of Pentecostal Theology* 17 (2000), pp. 81–95. 'The Moltmann-Pentecostal Dialogue: Implications for Mission', *Journal of Pentecostal Theology* 11.2 (2003), pp. 271–87.

To Asia Pacific Theological Seminary, P.O. Box 377, Baguio City 2600, Philippines, for: 'The Holy Spirit and Contextualisation', *Asian Journal of Pentecostal Studies* 4.2 (2001), pp. 201–13. 'A Charismatic Approach to other Faiths', *Asian Journal of Pentecostal Studies* 6.2 (2003).

I would also like to thank Cambridge University Press for permission to reproduce Figure 4.1, p. 106, from Jeremy S. Begbie, *Theology, Music and Time* (2000).

Title Description

This book develops a holistic charismatic theology of mission that is rooted in the pentecostal-charismatic tradition and yet contributes to the wider thinking on mission. The need for a holistic approach to mission has been widely acknowledged within Pentecostal and charismatic circles. Within wider debates the need for a pneumatological theology of mission has been recognised: one that builds on but goes beyond the significant work of David Bosch.

This book contains two parts. The first surveys both charismatic and wider Pentecostal understandings of mission, with the former focusing on experience in Britain as influenced by John Wimber. The importance of eschatology and contextualisation to a charismatic theology of mission are particularly noted. These themes are developed in the second part, which addresses different issues that need considering in a holistic theology of mission: the holistic content of mission; the experiential nature of mission; the contextual grounding of mission; the community focus of mission; and spirituality for mission. The book develops a holistic framework for understanding the 'mission of the Spirit' that contributes to both pentecostal and ecumenical thinking on mission. This mission is characterised by 'blessings' and 'yearnings' and in both we discover God at work by his Spirit growing the kingdom that centres on Jesus Christ.

1

Introduction

I have always had a fascination with the roots of the Christian faith and how it connects with the world. For a number of years there seemed no connection and hence faith seemed irrelevant and not worth bothering with. Then I rediscovered Jesus Christ within a charismatic community committed to reaching out into the world. At once faith became relevant, challenging and exciting. Being rooted in Christ and connected to the world came together for me in the experience of mission, both where I was and through visits to other parts of the world: encountering situations where people were reaching out in faith to transform people and communities following the example of Christ. I was inspired by missionaries whose deep personal faith and passion for reaching out to others challenged my own life and the direction in which I was going. This vision, glimpsed in different ways over the years as the Spirit has guided, led me to work with an inner-city church, then with the Church Mission Society (CMS) and now on to ordained ministry.

This vision of faith and mission has both enticed me on and yet also made me stop and question some of what passes for mission in our churches. Why do some people see mission simply in terms of evangelism when God's abundance embraces much more? Why do others see mission in intellectual rather than experiential terms? Why is there a reluctance to make the gospel contextually relevant? Why is mission sometimes seen in personal rather than community terms? Why are mission and spirituality considered separately? Theological study has helped me place such a vision and questions within a wider context and given me a language with which to explore ways forward. The charismatic tradition has been of great blessing to many of us and its insights on mission deserve a wider

But no are can understand you!

hearing. The theology developed here draws both on what is often termed the 'pentecostal-charismatic' tradition and also on wider insights in the theology of mission. The aim of this work is to develop a holistic charismatic theology of mission, shaped by the Spirit, rooted in Christ and seeking to embrace more of the fullness of God's working in the world.

The Pentecostal-Charismatic Tradition

There is much debate over the definition of 'pentecostal' with different people defining 'pentecostal identity' on certain experiential, theological and historical grounds. The difficulty is to be open to the great diversity of a movement that has grown rapidly and includes huge numbers of people across the world, and yet be able to speak meaningfully of particular groups and movements within the whole. Developing the approach of Walter Hollenweger, in this book I will use the term 'pentecostal' to encompass the worldwide movement within which we can identify three broad strands: Pentecostal, charismatic, and Locally Initiated Churches.[1] Here 'pentecostal' refers to the classical pentecostal churches such as the Assemblies of God. The term 'charismatic' encompasses the more recent charismatic movement within mainline churches and also neocharismatics, 'participants in independent, postdenominational, nondenominational, or indigenous groups or organizations',[2] and the 'Third Wave' movement. What I have termed Locally Initiated Churches, hereafter LICs, is an alternative term for David Barrett's 'Non-White indigenous churches' used by Hollenweger. Allan Anderson argues for this group to be treated differently from the former two from an African perspective and for the need to talk of 'initiated' rather than 'indigenous' (or 'independent' to use the

[1]   See W.J. Hollenweger, *Pentecostalism: Origins and Developments Worldwide* (Massachusetts: Hendrickson, 1997), 1–2. For a more detailed consideration of pentecostal identity from a similar perspective see Allan Anderson, *An Introduction to Pentecostalism* (Cambridge: Cambridge University Press, 2004), 9–15.

[2]   Stanley M. Burgess and Eduard M. van der Maas (eds.), *The New International Dictionary of Pentecostal and Charismatic Movements* (Grand Rapids: Zondervan, 2002), xxi.

older term) churches.[3] By using the term 'initiated' he stresses the local origins of the churches, as opposed to European mission-founded churches, many of which are moving towards becoming more 'indigenous'.

The pentecostal movement is characterised by certain experiences of the Holy Spirit, often referred to as the *charismata*, and I want to follow Amos Yong and others in suggesting that it is this that defines the unifying factor for the movement.[4] Within this broad picture the charismatic movement can be seen as having nine essential elements: a focus on Jesus, praise, love of the Bible, the belief that God speaks today, evangelism, awareness of evil, spiritual gifts, eschatological expectation and spiritual power.[5] Yet no definition can be based on experience separate from theology despite the tendency to separate experience and thought within the movement. There is a need to acknowledge and develop the theological characteristics of the movement in a way that relates to experience. This has been attempted by Donald Dayton, who outlines five cardinal doctrines from the early literature of the movement, and a more recent approach is that of Terry Cross.[6] The limitation of these is that they emphasise the Western evangelical roots of the movement and play down the non-Western and non-evangelical roots. They also neglect the need to bring tradition into the theological debate, for example in Cross's attempt to define theology in terms of the biblical narrative and experiential pentecostal narrative.[7] In this book I am taking for granted the existence of communities shaped by pentecostal and biblical narratives. I am also presuming a certain amount of doctrine that is shared by pentecos-

[3] Allan Anderson, *African Reformation: African Initiated Christianity in the 20th Century* (Asmara: Africa World Press, 2001), 4, 10–11.
[4] Amos Yong, *Discerning the Spirit(s): A Pentecostal-Charismatic Contribution to Christian Theology of Religions* (Sheffield: Sheffield Academic Press, 2000), 161.
[5] P.D. Hocken, 'Charismatic Movement' in Burgess and van der Maas (eds.), *Dictionary of Pentecostal and Charismatic Movements*, 515.
[6] Donald W. Dayton, *Theological Roots of Pentecostalism* (London: Scarecrow Press, 1987); Terry L. Cross, 'The Rich Feast of Theology: Can Pentecostals Bring the Main Course or Only the Relish?', *Journal of Pentecostal Theology* 16 (2000), 27–47.
[7] Cross, 'Rich Feast', 36.

tals and evangelicals, such as the focus on the cross of Christ. Rather
than repeat work done well elsewhere I want to stretch the thinking
of the movement in particular areas in the theology of mission. This
will be done through a recognition of the existing pentecostal and
charismatic traditions and through interactions with wider theological traditions.

Throughout this book I want to draw on the wide pentecostal
scholarship but develop a framework that is particularly charismatic.
This particularity comes out of my own experience as someone
whose faith has been shaped by the Holy Spirit at work in charismatic movements within the Church of England, notably through
the (often indirect) influence of David Pytches and Michael Mitton.
It will be seen in this book through my choice of sources and dialogue partners that reflect my own context and Anglican Church
involvement. I see this contextual nature to be a strength, and yet I
have resisted the temptation to address a purely Anglican, British
setting. The framework developed here is sufficiently broad to be
useful in reflecting on mission in other contexts.

Pentecostal Theology of Mission

The pentecostal movement has not been known for its theological
depth and as Frank Macchia notes, 'Pentecostals have generally felt
that Bible study and proclamation were sufficient to guide the
church in its fellowship and mission.'[8] Yet, as Douglas Jacobsen
points out, pentecostals have always sought to bring theology and
experience together even if their theological style differed from
other Christians.[9] However, it is perhaps only recently that pentecostals have sought to interact with wider theological scholarship.
In 1991 a pentecostal conference on World Evangelisation was held
at Brighton with the part intention of laying to rest 'the notion that

---

[8] Frank D. Macchia, 'The Struggle for Global Witness: Shifting Paradigms in Pentecostal Theology' in Murray W. Dempster, Byron D. Klaus
and Douglas Petersen (eds.), *The Globalization of Pentecostalism: A Religion
Made to Travel* (Oxford: Regnum, 1999), 8.

[9] Douglas Jacobsen, *Thinking in the Spirit: Theologies of the Early Pentecostal
Movement* (Bloomington: Indiana University Press, 2003), 3–8.

serious scholarly work is absent from the movement'.[10] In 1992 the *Journal of Pentecostal Theology (JPT)* was launched by Sheffield Academic Press together with a related supplementary series. Since then much critical reflection has been undertaken, although the reflection on the nature of mission seems less developed than other areas. It is still the case that we need to look back to 1985 for Paul Pomerville's assessment of the pentecostal contribution to the theology of mission.[11] Since then a number of detailed studies have addressed particular mission issues in some depth, but the time has come to draw some of the issues together.[12] This fits with the analysis of pentecostal missiology given by Grant McClung, who argues that a focus on mission as church growth has since the 1990s expanded to embrace evermore holistic concerns, particularly issues of culture and social responsibility.[13] Macchia makes the same point in his analysis of changing pentecostal paradigms in theology in which he argues for a move towards a holistic understanding of healing as embracing the whole of creation, and the need to move from 'a sectarian to an ecumenical witness'.[14] From a non-Western perspective this move towards a more integrated approach is in line with what Anderson terms the 'African Reformation' of Christianity by African Initiated Churches, which exhibits a 'holistic concern for the whole of life'.[15]

It has been argued that pentecostalism is more representative of an age that is passing and should not form the basis of a theology of mission for the future. There is a certain ambiguity here that David Martin summarises well:

---

[10] Harold D. Hunter and Peter D. Hocken (eds.), *All Together in One Place: Theological Papers from the Brighton Conference on World Evangelization* (Sheffield: Sheffield Academic Press, 1993), 11.

[11] Paul A. Pomerville, *The Third Force in Missions* (Massachusetts: Hendrickson, 1985).

[12] Examples here are Douglas Petersen on social involvement, *Not by Might Nor by Power: A Pentecostal Theology of Social Concern in Latin America* (Oxford: Regnum, 1996) and Yong on approaches to other faiths, *Discerning*.

[13] L. Grant McClung Jr, '"Try to Get People Saved": Revisiting the Paradigm of an Urgent Pentecostal Missiology' in Dempster, Klaus and Petersen (eds.), *Globalization of Pentecostalism*, 30–51.

[14] Macchia, 'Struggle'.

[15] Anderson, *African Reformation*, 256.

On the one hand you can, if you will, insist that Pentecostalism belongs to a wave of fundamentalism sweeping world religions in a last-ditch defence against modernity. Or you can see it as an adaptable form of heart-work and spiritual self-exploration breaking free of the restrictive protocols of enlightened reason into a New Age of post-modernity.[16]

He sees more evidence for the latter and speaks of how pentecostalism 'is sufficiently adaptable to forge links with very different social formations' and has now become a 'multi-centered' movement.[17] Pentecostalism thus has much to contribute to the discussion of mission in the contemporary world, even if self-critical reflection is required. Harvey Cox argues in a similar way that 'fundamentalism', in his view, is one negative response to contemporary world challenges, and what is needed is 'experientialism':

> for any religion to grow in today's world, it must possess two capabilities: it must be able to include and transform at least certain elements of preexisting religions which still retain a strong grip on the cultural subconscious. It must also equip people to live in rapidly changing societies where personal responsibility and inventiveness, skills associated with a democratic polity and an entrepreneurial economy, are indispensable.[18]

He wishes that pentecostalism were wholly committed to experientialism, but admits that deep tensions remain within the movement. I would challenge the either/or approach of Cox and, as I stated earlier, there is a need for a theological approach that is both rooted in the fundamentals of Christian faith and yet also adaptable and connected to experiences of the world in which we live. In seeking such an approach it seems appropriate to turn to the Holy Spirit as he both roots us in the truth and challenges us to go out into the world. Central to the theology of mission developed in this book is

---

[16] David Martin, *Pentecostalism: The World their Parish* (Oxford: Blackwell, 2002), 169.

[17] Ibid.

[18] Harvey Cox, *Fire from Heaven: The Rise of Pentecostal Spirituality and the Reshaping of Religion in the 21st Century* (London: Cassell, 1996), 218–19.

a framework centred around movements of the Holy Spirit that draws on existing pentecostal insights on mission.

Wider Theology of Mission

A common place to start in considering the theology of mission is the definitive work of David Bosch, *Transforming Mission*. Writing in 1991, he argues that there has been a growing crisis in mission that is evidence of the church undergoing a paradigm shift in its understanding and practice of mission. Outlining changes in culture, Bosch writes of the emergence of a postmodern mission paradigm and it is vital to take on board the challenges he gives to mission thinking today. He argues that what is needed is: (1) 'the indispensableness of conviction and commitment' and (2) to 'retrieve togetherness, interdependence, "symbiosis"'.[19] The emerging paradigm must embrace 'both the centrifugal and the centripetal forces' in a 'creative tension'.[20] Whilst giving a comprehensive summary of mission thinking and key challenges for the future, it has been questioned as to what extent Bosch carries through more recent thinking in mission. In a significant critique, Kirsteen Kim praises Bosch's work for its summary of mission thinking, but argues that it reflects more of the old paradigm rather than setting the agenda for the new. In particular she feels that Bosch neglects the concerns of feminism, ecology and indigenous spiritualities and this reflects the lack of an adequate pneumatology underlying the whole work. She contrasts the book with the World Council of Churches assembly in Canberra in the same year, 1991. Under the title 'Come, Holy Spirit – Renew the Whole Creation' the debate concentrated on the 'action of the Spirit within and outside the church, and on the criteria necessary to recognise the presence of the Spirit'.[21] Kim concludes her argument by saying that 'The post-modern paradigm

---

[19] David Bosch, *Transforming Mission: Paradigm Shifts in Theology of Mission* (New York: Orbis, 1991), 362.

[20] Ibid., 367. For an exploration of this theme in Bosch and evangelical mission theology see John Corrie, 'Creative Tensions in the Mission of the Church: David Bosch Ten Years On', *ANVIL* 18.2 (2001), 97–106.

[21] Emilio Castro, 'Editorial', *ER* 43.2 (April 1991), 163, quoted in Kirsteen Kim, 'Post-Modern Mission: A Paradigm Shift in David Bosch's

will take into account not only the Spirit of mission but also the mission of the Spirit.'[22]

I think this distinction between the 'Spirit of mission' and the 'mission of the Spirit' is a key differential in approaches to mission. Most approaches, even within pentecostal and evangelical circles, prefer the former and yet there is a need to move to the latter. For example, a fairly recent consideration of the Holy Spirit and mission from the Evangelical Missiological Society starts with a consideration of mission and then goes on to ask the question: what is the Spirit's role in missions?[23] Although comments are made to the effect that the mission is the Spirit's this overall line of thinking from mission to the Spirit seems to dominate. What is needed is an approach that asks the question: what might mission look like if we start with the work of the Spirit? What would a Spirit-shaped mission look like? In answering that question the 'creative tension' that Bosch identified needs to be central. This book takes such an approach, outlining a framework for mission that is based on a set of movements of the Holy Spirit. These movements are between the 'particular' (individuals and communities) and the 'universal' (those that forever open us up to others and creation, making us aware of our interdependence), stating in different terms the tension that Bosch identifies. Visually, we can represent this framework as follows:

This framework draws on pentecostal theology of mission, in focus-

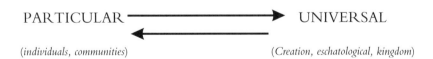

Mission of the Spirit

PARTICULAR ⟶ UNIVERSAL

⟵

(individuals, communities)   *(Creation, eschatological, kingdom)*

ing on the work of the Holy Spirit, and yet is sensitive to the 'creative tension' that is significant in wider theologies of mission. Thus

---

[21] *(continued)* Theology of Mission' in Timothy Yates (ed.), *Mission – An Invitation to God's Future* (Sheffield: Cliff College, 2000), 102.

[22] Kim, 'Post-Modern Mission', 108.

[23] C. Douglas McConnell (ed.), *The Holy Spirit and Mission Dynamics* (Pasadena: William Carey Library, 1997).

it represents a new model of mission that should contribute to both charismatic and the wider theology of mission.

Blessed Yearning

It has often struck me how much energy we put into the *meaning* of mission without giving weight to the *character* of mission. It is difficult to motivate mission through preaching and teaching the meaning of mission alone – somehow we have to make the character of mission attractive. Tim Naish speaks of the attention given to mission theory yet wonders if theory alone is sufficient for our postmodern context. Should we not instead work through metaphor and symbol, which stimulate the imagination and the spirit, as well as the intellect? Presenting the character of mission through images can bring concepts together in a motivating way. Also, an image offers the possibility of both flexibility and clarity, being '*open and broad* enough to sustain a variety of interpretation and development, whilst remaining *definite and narrow* enough to provide a focus and evocative meaning'.[24] Tomlinson echoes others in suggesting that metaphor and the development of the imagination may provide a way forward in theological education.[25] The framework I am suggesting builds on the three metaphors: 'particular', 'universal' and movement. These have been given some meaning above, but I am deliberately allowing a wider variety of interpretation to develop through this book before bringing the ideas together in the conclusion. These three metaphors seem usefully to encompass a variety of debates within the theology of mission, although the first two may be admittedly abstract when presented in most local church settings. Hence, I want also to develop through this book the two metaphors of 'blessing' and 'yearning' which can be seen to characterise the mission movement of the Spirit.

These metaphors will run often beneath the surface of the book and will at times break out into the open. They most easily relate to

[24] Tim Naish, 'Ways Forward in Mission Studies: Theory or Image?', *Missiology* 27.2 (1999), 166.
[25] Anne L. Tomlinson, *Training God's Spies: Developing the Imagination in Theological Formation* (Edinburgh: Contact Pastoral Trust, 2001).

everyday human and charismatic experience and to any understanding of the Holy Spirit based on the story of Pentecost and the
eschatological passage of Romans 8:18–30. These help fill out an
initial meaning for our metaphors: a mission of blessing is based on
the nature of the God of gracious blessing. This is seen at Pentecost
as the nations hear the 'wonders of God' proclaimed to them and
the eschatological kingdom is seen breaking into the world. These
blessings are conveyed by the Spirit and we can see Christians and
churches filled to overflowing with the love of God in a way that
may sometimes seem like a transcendent feast, a lavish welcome into
the kingdom of God that cannot but lead to praise and joy. There is
a great sense of power in this blessing of the Spirit, but it is a power
that is directed outwards and not just inwards. It is the power that
cannot but lead to witness, a witness that is holistic in nature. There
is an outpouring of evangelistic witness to Jesus as Christ that draws
more people into God's feast of blessings. There is a deep witness to
the liberating freedom of the kingdom that God desires all people to
enter into. It is a witness without boundaries, which must eventually encompass the whole of creation.

   Yet this abundance of blessing cannot be separated from the reality of a world experiencing 'yearnings' of many kinds. The whole of
creation 'groans' in its knowledge that the fullness of blessings has
'not yet' come, that there is still a bondage to sin that brings
brokenness and hurt in so many ways. Deep sighs of sorrow and
weariness continue to express despair and hopelessness, exile from
the promised land. There is always a yearning for more that may
lead to a fresh turning to God, and a deep repentance over the ways
things are personally, in our communities, in our nations and in our
world. Yearning may lead to blessing and for that we praise God,
but it may lead to further yearnings that are as yet unsatisfied and
express something of the groanings of the Spirit as he searches
the desert experiences of this world. The mission of the Spirit can
be seen as that of yearning within the world and bringing blessings
into the world. It is a mission that embraces the whole of creation
and the ordinary of life in all its diversity. Yet it is also a mission
characterised by the inbreaking blessings of God that make a difference and usher in tastes of the kingdom to come. Our task is to 'live
in the Spirit', to develop a 'mission spirituality', by which we are
caught up in the mission of the Spirit. In such a spirituality we will

continually find ourselves directed, guided and sent into the world to feel its sense of yearning and to see outbreaks of blessing. In this we will taste the sufferings and resurrection of Jesus as the Spirit leads us ever deeper into his life alongside the life of the world.

Further details of this charismatic approach to mission are worked out in the remainder of this book, but there are two important implications of this approach that need to be emphasised at the start. First, this approach challenges tendencies to triumphalism and imperialism. Because of the dramatic growth of the pentecostal-charismatic movement worldwide, estimated at going 'from zero to almost 500 million in less than a century', there is a tendency for pentecostals to triumphalism.[26] Gary McGee, himself a pentecostal, challenges the movement to go beyond the rather simplistic use of statistics to justify its approach to mission. Instead the movement needs to 'face the issues', notably the need for theological reflection and appreciation of the social aspects of mission highlighted especially in the Third World.[27] An emphasis on the yearning of the Spirit provides a counter-balance to triumphalism, stressing the fact that not all mission 'succeeds' and we never get beyond our incompleteness in this world. The mission of the Spirit highlights the need for humility and should dissuade us from claiming the glory for any of the works of God.

Secondly, any Western writer on mission also faces the uncomfortable charge of 'imperialism', which is based particularly on some of the happenings of the missionary movement. The term 'imperialism' needs careful definition, as Brian Stanley argues, and it is not possible to label all mission as negatively imperialistic.[28] However, there is a temptation to adopt a position of the superiority of our understanding of mission and the 'gospel' (which incorporates cultural understandings) over that of others. The approach to mission being suggested here is based on common yearnings that are shared by all people in all places – we all stand on common ground. It is within

---

[26] Hollenweger, *Pentecostalism*, 1.

[27] Gary B. McGee, 'Pentecostal Missiology: Moving Beyond Triumphalism to Face the Issues', *PNEUMA* 16.2 (1994), 278–81.

[28] Brian Stanley, *The Bible and the Flag: Protestant Missions and British Imperialism in the Nineteenth and Twentieth Centuries* (Leicester: Inter-Varsity Press, 1990).

and as a result of these yearnings that we see the blessings that the Holy Spirit brings into the world. There is a great diversity of yearnings and blessings and which we recognise and highlight will depend on our own particular experience of the Spirit. This book aims confidently to outline some of the yearnings and blessings that have been discovered from within the charismatic tradition, but without therefore implying that none other are possible or desirable. Let us commit ourselves to the truth and wisdom of the Holy Spirit as we seek to immerse ourselves more deeply in God's mission in the world.

This book is organised in two parts. The first reviews current mission thinking within the charismatic and wider pentecostal traditions, in chapters 2 and 3. The second part of the book seeks to develop a holistic charismatic theology of mission that addresses the questions posed at the start of this book. Chapter 4 argues for the holistic nature of mission through an exploration of eschatology. Chapter 5 argues that holistic mission needs to embrace all of our experiences through an examination of a dialogue between pentecostals and Jürgen Moltmann. Chapter 6 extends this to consider the question of contextualisation, with particular reference to what holistic mission might mean in the context of other faiths. Holistic mission can only be carried out in community and Chapter 7 develops thinking on voluntary communities to suggest the essential characteristics of charismatic mission communities. Consideration is also given as to how these communities interact and relate to church structures. Holistic mission needs to embrace both thinking and practice, and so in Chapter 8 the outline of a charismatic mission spirituality is developed. In concluding, Chapter 9 draws together the different aspects of the framework that have been developed throughout the book and considers some of the challenges that need to be taken forward.

Part 1

CURRENT THINKING

handwritten margin notes:

— what about non-Anglican traditional denominations?

— what about the new charismatic churches / denominational networks?

Chapters 2+3 follow will Theological / Technical language.

2

Charismatic Theology of Mission

I anticipated training in spiritual warfare and equipping to advance the kingdom of God. I envisioned Christians coming together, singing and praying, receiving encouragement or exhortation from scripture, then dispersing throughout Orange County, California, to perform dramatic healings, expel demonic spirits, oppose evil authorities. Then, I thought, we would return later in the day with new converts and reports of great miracles, overflowing with joy and worshipping God.[1]

As a one-time missionary I often preached on the 'Great Commission' found in Matthew 28:18–20. I thought I had squeezed every drop of teaching one could out of those tremendous verses. It is only during the last fourteen years or so that I have begun to realise that in fact I had totally overlooked one of the major dimensions of the text. Jesus had told his disciples to make other disciples, baptise them and teach them '*to obey everything I have commanded you*'. I see now that this '*everything*' included a ministry of 'signs and wonders'. Every time the kingdom was preached by the disciples they would minister in 'signs and wonders'. This was what Jesus had taught them to do.[2]

John Wimber, as a new Christian, read the New Testament and became excited by the vision of the church presented there, and thus anticipated great blessings when he first attended a church service.

---

[1] John Wimber and Kevin Springer, *Power Evangelism* (London: Hodder & Stoughton, 1985), 13.

[2] David Pytches, *Come, Holy Spirit* (London: Hodder & Stoughton, 1995), 1.

Sadly, the reality did not match the anticipation and this gap between current experience and that of the first disciples motivated
much of Wimber's theology and desire to train others. David
Pytches describes Wimber's first visit to his church as a time of
'wonderful blessing' in which a model for every Christian to minister in the power of the Holy Spirit was demonstrated.[3] This built on
Pytches' earlier realisation that as a missionary he had omitted from
his reading of the Great Commission the need for 'signs and wonders'. The charismatic movement of the 1980s was captured by a
vision of the blessings of the kingdom and a yearning for churches to
be trained to bring these blessings into reality in the life of the
church and the world.

John Wimber's Theology of Mission

This chapter seeks to outline existing charismatic theologies of mission through the key figure of Wimber, whose theology is largely
followed by Pytches, and through a focus on Anglican charismatics
in England. The key figure of Wimber provides a link with wider
charismatic thinking and as such he is a good person to begin with.
Fundamental to Wimber's outlook was a commitment to evangelism which developed from personal evangelism into a wider desire
for church planting as a means to evangelism.[4] 'Signs and wonders'
became a part of Wimber's understanding of church life, but they
were not to be seen as an end in themselves, only as part of the resources for evangelism.[5] His shift in this direction came partly from
an awareness of the pentecostal movement in Latin America as mediated through C. Peter Wagner's book *Look Out! The Pentecostals
are Coming.*[6] Wimber became aware of the limitations of his 'secu-
larised Western worldview' and he later argued strongly that our
Western worldview needs correcting if we are to see and appreciate

---

[3] David Pytches (ed.), *John Wimber: His Influence and Legacy* (Guildford:
Eagle, 1998), 33–4.
[4] Ibid., 9.
[5] Eddie Gibbs, 'The Evangelist' in Pytches (ed.), *John Wimber,* 78–9.
[6] See, C. Peter Wagner, *Spiritual Power and Church Growth* (London:
Hodder & Stoughton, 1986), 9.

spiritual power, building on the work of Paul Hiebert and Charles Kraft.[7]

The essential theological theme that held Wimber's theology together was the 'Kingdom of God' and the gospel to be proclaimed was 'a call to the King and his kingdom'.[8] The aims of 'signs and wonders' was 'to confront people with [Jesus'] message that *in him* the kingdom had come, and that they had to decide to accept or reject it'.[9] In his understanding of the 'kingdom' Wimber was largely influenced by the work of George Ladd, particularly in his understanding of 'two ages':

> In brief, this age, which extends from creation to the Day of the Lord … is the age of human existence in weakness and mortality, of evil, sin, and death. The Age to Come will see the realization of all that the reign of God means, and will be the age of resurrection into eternal life in the Kingdom of God.[10]

At the present time Wimber sees us as 'caught between two ages' and in the life of Jesus we see how the 'future age, the kingdom of God, invaded the present age, the realm of Satan'.[11] The context of Christian life and mission is therefore one of battle. We are:

> thrust into the middle of a battle with Satan: it's a tug-of-war, and the prize is the souls of men and women. Satan's captivity of men and women has many facets, but denying them final salvation is his primary goal … Our mission is to rescue those who have been taken captive as a result of Adam's fall.[12]

---

[7] John Wimber and Kevin Springer, *Power Evangelism* (London: Hodder & Stoughton, 1992), 129–54; Charles Kraft, *Christianity with Power: Experiencing the Supernatural* (London: Marshall Pickering, 1990).

[8] Wimber and Springer, *Power Evangelism*, 36.

[9] Ibid., 30.

[10] George Ladd, *A Theology of the New Testament* (Guildford: Lutterworth Press, 1974), 48, quoted in Wimber and Springer, *Power Evangelism* (1992), 31.

[11] Wimber and Springer, *Power Evangelism*, 33.

[12] Ibid., 44.

This battle will require 'power encounters' in which the kingdom of Satan is overcome by the power of God in order for the gospel to be believed. Evangelism will require such power encounters if it is to be effective. In terms of the framework of this book, we can understand Wimber's theology of mission as being rooted in a movement of the Spirit from the eschatological kingdom into the present, centred on Jesus and seen in conversion, signs and wonders.

This understanding of mission as a battle and God as the aggressor is balanced in Wimber's thinking with a stress on the mercy of God. This stress is prominent in his book on healing in which he describes how his convictions from Scripture were augmented by a profound vision of God's mercy. The vision was of a 'honeycomb [in the sky] with honey dripping out on to people below', which some people received and others rejected. The interpretation Wimber felt God give was that this was an image of God's mercy. 'For some people it's a blessing, but for others it's a hindrance. There's plenty for everyone.'[13] This mercy, grace or healing is seen as great enough to touch every area of life and God's mercy 'should always be communicated in love and gentleness, warmth and compassion'.[14] This healing Wimber relates to the promise of 2 Corinthians 5:17 that 'we are a new creation: the old has gone, the new has come!'[15] The emphasis on God's mercy provided a motivation for personal healing and also for social work, notably the 'Mercy ministries' of the Vineyard churches that 'were latterly distributing thousands of dollars' worth of food to the poor on a regular basis'.[16]

For Wimber, mission involves a battle with Satan in the power of the Holy Spirit in order that the blessings of God's kingdom may be known and people come to know the King, Jesus. But mission is not about continual, automatic blessings and may well include times when blessings remain absent, despite being longed after. In my terms, mission involves yearning as well as blessing. Wimber offers himself as a particular example of this in regard to the healing

---

[13] John Wimber and Kevin Springer, *Power Healing* (London: Hodder & Stoughton, 1986), 70.
[14] Ibid., 82.
[15] Ibid., 88.
[16] Pytches (ed.), *John Wimber*, 28.

ministry. He speaks of a 'long struggle' that involved a 'ten-month period of ineffectual prayer' before he saw any healings.[17] This he saw later in positive terms:

> This period of failure was a learning experience, a time in which I was purged of my pride and self-sufficiency. I was humiliated, and I was humbled. God had first to cleanse a vessel before it was fit to fill with his precious oil of healing. I believe God began healing the sick through me only after I came to a place of total dependence on his grace and mercy. I also learnt about total obedience to God's word.[18]

Later Wimber talks of his heart complaint that despite much prayer was not healed.[19] In asking why some people are not healed he appeals to the 'already and the not yet' seen in Romans 8:18–25. He concludes his book by saying that we have to be content with 'knowing in part' (1 Cor. 13:12) whilst waiting for the 'fullness of the kingdom of God' that is coming.[20] Unsatisfied yearnings are a part of the experience of mission.

Wimber's understanding of mission is integrated with a spirituality for mission. The Christian life is to be lived in an attitude of prayerful waiting (yearning) and discerning of what God the Father is doing. Once discerned then action needs to follow that 'blesses what the Father is doing'. This is contrasted with an approach that sets out in mission and then asks God to bless what has been planned: 'we must learn to wait on God, allowing him to speak, act, lead'.[21] This is something that David Pytches also notes and links both with the ministry of Jesus and the practice of 'spiritual gifts'.[22] God is the initiator of mission and the spiritual gifts are 'expressions of God's grace at work' that help us see what God is doing.[23] It is within this context that we can understand the importance of worship for mission in the ministry of Wimber, whose background was

---

[17] Wimber and Springer, *Power Healing*, 72.
[18] Ibid.
[19] Ibid., 159–62.
[20] Ibid., 246.
[21] Wimber and Springer, *Power Evangelism*, 150.
[22] Pytches (ed.), *John Wimber*, 28; Pytches, *Come, Holy Spirit*, 40–52.
[23] Pytches, *Come, Holy Spirit*, 47.

as a musician. The Vineyard 'liturgy' of worship, word and ministry places the ministry of mission in the context of giving to God in worship and receiving from God through his word. This link between mission and worship is significant but remains in need of further charismatic exploration. James Steven argues that charismatic worship reflects an appropriate inculturation with modern society that is attractive as a part of mission.[24] Chris Cocksworth outlines charismatic worship within a Trinitarian doctrinal outlook within which mission flows out of our worship as we participate in the life of the Trinitarian God.[25] In many ways the Wimber–Pytches approach picks up the developing emphasis in the theology of mission on *missio Dei*, 'the shift toward understanding mission is *God's mission*'.[26] This approach is not greatly developed theologically but practically it reflects the wider theology that articulates the understanding that 'To participate in mission is to participate in the movement of God's love toward people, since God is a fountain of sending love.'[27] Wimber and Pytches give a practical outworking of such a theology.

It is worth noting a number of critiques of this theology of mission, although I want to address these more later when constructing an alternative theology of mission. First, the emphasis on *missio Dei* has led many to a much wider understanding of God's working in the world. For Wimber and Pytches it is about God's initiative *in the church* in directing its mission, but since the International Missionary Council meeting at Willingen in 1952 *missio Dei* has increasingly been about God's initiatives in mission *in the history of the world*. God's mission is greater than the church's mission and the Holy Spirit is at work in the world.[28] There is a notable lack of such an understanding of the Holy Spirit in the work of Wimber and Pytches. Secondly, the focus on two opposing kingdoms can lead to an unhealthy dualism with too much profile

---

[24] James H.S. Steven, *Worship in the Spirit: Charismatic Worship in the Church of England* (Carlisle: Paternoster Press, 2002), 210–13.
[25] Christopher Cocksworth, *Holy, Holy, Holy: Worshipping the Trinitarian God* (London: Darton, Longman & Todd, 1997).
[26] Bosch, *Transforming Mission*, 389.
[27] Ibid., 390.
[28] Ibid., 390–92.

being given to the work of Satan. Nigel Wright argues that to see
the world as simply Satan's territory seems to ignore the category of
'the natural'.[29] As one person put it, 'Is it possible to have a cold in
peace without it being a spiritual issue?'[30] Andrew Walker argues
that the charismatic outlook can lead to the perception of a
'paranoid universe' in which the work of demons seems always
threatening.[31] He feels that the pentecostal movement avoided this
by an evangelistic and Christ-centred approach, yet does not
appreciate these emphases in the life and teaching of Wimber and
other charismatics. Thirdly, there seems a separation between
understanding the kingdom of God and works of mercy which
surely belong together. Also, issues of social justice and ecological
concern seem absent from a mission which focuses on evangelism.
We will return to the nature of our experience of God in the church
and world and our understanding of the kingdom and mission in
chapters 4 and 5. Before then it is important to broaden our
understanding of charismatic theology of mission through what
came before and after Wimber and through parallel developments
in the wider pentecostal theology of mission.

Early Charismatic Theology of Mission

The theology of mission of Wimber and Pytches develops some,
but not all, of the themes present in earlier charismatic theology of
mission. In this section I want to outline the theology of mission of
three key leaders from the 1960s and 1970s: Michael Harper, David
Watson and John Gunstone.

   Michael Harper became one of the key leaders in the early charismatic movement. As a curate at the influential evangelical church
of All Souls, Langham Place, during the 1960s he was 'filled with all

---

[29]   Nigel Wright, 'The Theology and Methodology of "Signs and Wonders"' in Tom Smail, Andrew Walker and Nigel Wright, *Charismatic Renewal: The Search for a Theology* (London: SPCK, 1993), 73–5.
[30]   Quoted in ibid., 75.
[31]   Tom Smail, 'The Devil you Think you Know: Demonology and the
Charismatic Movement' in Smail, Walker and Wright, *Charismatic Renewal*, 88–90.

the fullness of God'[32] and found his ministry transformed. Through contact with others he began to interpret his experience within the pentecostal framework of baptism in the Spirit. Harper shared his experience with churches and eventually in 1964 set up the Fountain Trust to encourage Christians around the country to experience the power of the Holy Spirit. Harper later established SOMA, the Sharing of Ministries Abroad, to help encourage Anglican churches around the world to experience the power of the Holy Spirit. David Watson experienced the 'filling of the Spirit' whilst a curate in Cambridge.[33] He already had many contacts in the evangelical world and had a growing reputation as an evangelist. Watson's experience of the Spirit led him into controversy with evangelical friends who opposed charismatic experiences.[34] Yet his experience of seeing his church grow dramatically in York, coupled with leading national and international missions, soon made him a recognised leader in the charismatic movement. John Gunstone received the baptism in the Spirit in 1964 and 'was later to become the most articulate spokesman for the charismatic movement in the more catholic wing of the Church of England'.[35]

Michael Harper provided a theology of mission focused on the 'kingdom of God' similar to that of Wimber but with a broader understanding. In *Walk in the Spirit*, published in 1968 during his time with the Fountain Trust, he draws out key themes learnt from the early charismatic movement in Britain. Mission is about the rule of God challenging the rule of Satan: 'We are fighting in enemy-held territory. Satan snipes at us from every direction. There are enemy agents everywhere. The enemy has immense power and resources, and numerous allies.'[36] For Harper the activity of Satan is 'massive and powerful', hindering people from meeting God. Mission

---

[32] P.D. Hocken, *Streams of Renewal: The Origins and Early Development of the Charismatic Movement in Great Britain* (Carlisle: Paternoster Press, 1997), 86.

[33] David Watson, *You are my God* (London: Hodder & Stoughton, 1983), 54.

[34] Teddy Saunders and Hugh Sansom, *David Watson: A Biography* (London: Hodder & Stoughton, 1992), 76–85.

[35] Hocken, *Streams of Renewal*, 109.

[36] Michael Harper, *Walk in the Spirit* (London: Hodder & Stoughton, 1968), 49.

involves liberating people from the power of Satan, and in this task the power of the Holy Spirit is crucial. People need to seek the power of the Spirit for themselves to become an effective part of this task.

This liberation from Satan takes four main forms in Harper's view: evangelism, healing, deliverance and social concern. This represents a broad understanding of the nature of mission. In each of these areas Harper focuses on how the Spirit enables believers to overcome Satan and so extend the kingdom of God. Thus in regard to evangelism the Spirit guides the evangelists, giving them the words and compassion they need in order to break the chains that bind 'Satan's captives'[37] and opening their eyes to the truth of Jesus. In healing the Spirit releases people from Satan's power over the body, although Harper is careful not to equate all illness with the work of Satan. In deliverance the Spirit releases people from demon-possession or from 'bondages' where Satan has gained a foothold in someone's life. In social concern the Spirit destroys racial barriers, reconciles people and gives the prophetic insight necessary to pursue issues of 'justice, public morality, and the plight of the under-nourished and under-privileged'.[38] These four forms of mission seem to reflect the wider debate in evangelical circles concerning the relationship between evangelism and social action.[39] Harper argues for both to be appreciated and augments them with the healing and deliverance emphases from the pentecostal movement.

Reflecting a decade later, Harper moves slightly away from the language of liberation from Satan, but maintains similar themes. Writing in 1979, Harper then saw the basic theological position of charismatic renewal as being 'that God, who invaded our world in the person of Jesus Christ nearly two thousand years ago, and who will come again "in like manner" sometime in the future, still actively moves amongst his people, and the effects of that real

---

[37] Ibid., 52.

[38] Ibid., 60.

[39] See the debate leading up to Lausanne I, the evangelical conference for World Evangelization held in 1974, discussed in a wider context by Robert T. Coote 'Lausanne II and World Evangelization,' *International Bulletin of Missionary Research* 14 (1990), 10–17.

presence are to be expected and experienced in our own lives'.[40]
Harper felt that the effect of charismatic renewal on evangelicals has
moved them from a judgmental attitude to the world to a compassion for the world. He also notes that charismatics have
rediscovered the itinerant ministry, the freedom to travel as moved
by the Holy Spirit, sharing their good news and bringing 'renewal
to every corner of the globe'.[41]

David Watson's entry into the charismatic renewal came out of a
longing for life in the church, and in the context of groups around
the country praying for revival.[42] His theological questioning focused on what 'baptism in the Spirit' meant, and whether the gifts of
the Spirit, particularly tongues, were for today.[43] For Watson evangelism was 'the foremost task of the church, next to worship' and
was of 'greater urgency than issues raised by the "charismatic" or ecumenical movements'.[44] Evangelism was primary and charismatic
issues were secondary – he was first and foremost an evangelist and
his theology of mission reflects this. In many ways his theology appears to be that inherited from the evangelicals of his day, reworked
to include the influence of the Spirit in all aspects of the task. His
book *I Believe in Evangelism* starts with the social context of people,
which demands that the church 'preach the gospel of Christ … by
word and deed, by the power of signs and wonders, and by the
power of the Holy Spirit'.[45] Watson sees the gospel as centring on
the kingdom, the authority and rule of God, with a need to preach
for a personal response. This was in line with evangelical thinking
but with more of an emphasis on the kingdom rather than the cross.
For Watson 'the Spirit of God is essentially a witnessing Spirit'[46]
who comes mainly to make us more effective in witness and evangelism. We are weak, but the Spirit guides our evangelism, gives
power to our witness, leads people to the truth of the gospel and

---

[40] Michael Harper, *This is the Day: A Fresh Look at Christian Unity* (London: Hodder & Stoughton, 1979), 57.

[41] Ibid., 71.

[42] Watson, *You are my God*, 49–53.

[43] Ibid., 56–64.

[44] David Watson, *I Believe in Evangelism* (London: Hodder & Stoughton, 1976), 11.

[45] Quoting Romans 15:18–19. Ibid., 24.

[46] Ibid., 169.

effects conversion.[47] Our need as evangelists is to come to God and receive the Holy Spirit and the need of people generally is to repent, believe and receive the Holy Spirit.[48]

During the 1970s Watson pioneered city-wide festivals of faith which focused on reconciliation, renewal and evangelism: reconciliation between churches and races; renewal of spiritual life especially through worship; and many forms of evangelism.[49] In this his vision of mission was widening to include worship and social issues, although still with evangelism primary.[50] The emphasis on worship within which the filling of the Spirit was often experienced perhaps replaced the pentecostal stress on 'baptism in the Spirit', a term Watson understood in relation to water baptism. For Watson, as also for Harper and Gunstone, it is the encounter with the sending God by his Spirit in worship that is at the heart of mission: people need to thirst for and receive the power of the Spirit which will naturally cause them to go out in mission. Effective mission is dependent upon a personal encounter with God the Holy Spirit.

This theme of worship was central to John Gunstone's understanding of mission: 'worship and mission are not two separate aspects of the Church's life but one'.[51] Spiritual renewal is about a fresh encounter with God, often in the context of worship. This encounter with God cannot but lead to mission, for 'the message of the Gospel is that the Father sends the Son and, in turn, Jesus sends his disciples in the power of the Holy Spirit'.[52] An encounter with God is an encounter with the one who sends us out in mission and as we go out there will be 'signs following'.[53] Gunstone picks out two particular signs: as a result of a fresh encounter with God in worship congregations should be 'used to bring the healing power of Jesus Christ to a sick world' and in 'helping people to live responsibly in

---

[47] Ibid., 171–8.

[48] Watson's three steps in leading people to Christian faith. Ibid., 77–80.

[49] These themes are explored in more detail by Matthew Porter, *David Watson: Evangelism, Renewal, Reconciliation* (Cambridge: Grove, 2003).

[50] Watson, *You are my God*, 179ff.

[51] John Gunstone, *A People for His Praise: Renewal and Congregational Life* (London: Hodder & Stoughton, 1978), 111.

[52] Ibid.

[53] A common expression in charismatic circles, echoing the New Testament signs of the apostles (e.g. 2 Cor. 12:12). Ibid., 122.

our multi-racial society'. In healing Gunstone includes caring for drug addicts, those suffering alcoholism and emotional break-downs, and deals with physical and emotional healing in a separate section on church healing services. Multi-racial concern springs from the Spirit being poured out on all peoples and Gunstone suggests that 'the local anti-race committee should be the place for as powerful a manifestation of the Holy Spirit as the charismatic prayer meeting'.[54] Thus Gunstone has a more positive view of the world than might be seen in, say, Harper, but he is careful to distinguish his theology of mission from that of the social gospel popular in the training colleges of the 1960s. There mission was seen to take its agenda from the world around, whereas Gunstone sees it taking its agenda first from God. A charismatic approach to social issues 'seeks to be sensitive to those concerns which the Lord himself sets before his Church ... Relevance in mission begins with God' not with the relevance to society.[55]

Reflecting his Anglo-Catholic roots Gunstone stresses that the result of mission is the church: 'the Church does not "have" a mission. Rather, the mission of Jesus Christ creates the church.'[56] Thus when Gunstone was thinking with others about mission on a new housing estate, rather than start with a church building and priest, they suggested buying two houses for Christian families and trust that they 'would have the necessary spiritual gifts for this missionary task and would be the beginnings of new congregations'.[57] A decade later, when reflecting on the ministry of John Wimber, Gunstone again comments that 'Church building is the prerogative of the Lord.' He feels that charismatics 'did not see the need for a critical review of the theological position of our church'. He feels that charismatics 'made efforts to interpret Pentecostal spirituality within the categories of our own traditions' without asking if more was needed, with denominational definitions needing changing.[58]

---

[54]   Ibid., 122–3.
[55]   Ibid., 124.
[56]   Ibid., 117.
[57]   Ibid., 121.
[58]   John Gunstone, *Signs and Wonders: The Wimber Phenomenon* (London: Daybreak, 1989), 119–21.

Contemporary Charismatic Theology of Mission

In summary, I have suggested that the early charismatic theology of mission centred on blessings received and shared. Blessings were received through a 'baptism in the Spirit' and the community experience of worship, and were shared with the world through mission. A movement from the eschatological kingdom into particular situations led to an outward movement into the world. Keeping a focus on evangelism, mission was re-envisioned around the theme of the 'kingdom of God', which was seen as including evangelism, healing, social action, overcoming divisions, and 'signs and wonders'. For some a holistic liberation from Satan was key to the extension of the kingdom, whereas for others the world was seen in a more positive way. Yearning is present in that the kingdom is 'now and not yet'. Thinking about ecclesiology did develop but perhaps without significant interaction with the ecclesiology of others within the same denomination. The charismatic theology of mission of the 1980s saw a more focused understanding of the kingdom and more developed approaches to personal spirituality. From the 1990s we can perhaps identify three strands in the theology of mission that overlap yet illustrate different emphases.[59] These strands are Revivalist, Contextual and Catholic with emphases on evangelism, life and spirituality. Mark Stibbe, who followed David Pytches as vicar at St Andrew's Church, Chorleywood, is a leading Anglican charismatic theologian, preacher and writer on the theme of revival. He links revival to mission through a focus on evangelism and the proclamation of the gospel: 'Revival is a season ordained by God in which the Holy Spirit awakens the Church to evangelise the lost, and the lost to their dire need of Jesus Christ.'[60] The theme of revival brings together those of mercy and kingdom we have seen in the

---

[59] Here I am drawing on the more detailed work found in Andrew M. Lord, 'Contextualisation in Britain: Insights from a Celtic Spirituality', MA dissertation (Birmingham, 1999); Gavin Wakefield, 'Mission in the Spirit: Revivalist and Celtic Strands of Mission', *ANVIL* 18.1 (2001), 7–20. I am not suggesting that these strands stand in isolation from one another and the people I mention have worked alongside others from differing strands. I am offering a model of understanding the differing emphases that exist in charismatic theology of mission.

[60] Mark Stibbe, *Revival* (Crowborough: Monarch, 1998), 14.

theology of Wimber.[61] Mission originates in the compassionate heart of God, which is communicated to the church through the Holy Spirit. The essence of this mission involves the proclamation of the gospel of the kingdom with the desire that individuals may be converted to God in Jesus Christ. Out from this narrow focus springs a movement that affects society, transforming wider morality.[62] But for Stibbe the work of the Spirit in the world is primarily one of bringing all to salvation through faith in Christ. The world is seen primarily in a negative light, as the kingdom of darkness that is 'pushed back' as the kingdom of God advances.[63] Stibbe's theology of mission can be seen as a natural development of that of Wimber/Pytches, which focuses on evangelism whilst occasionally hinting at a larger kingdom and work of the Spirit in the world.[64] A similar understanding of revival focused on encounter with God, evangelism and an impacted society is seen in the writings of Nicky Gumbel, pioneer of the Alpha course.[65]

Following a very different approach, various authors who stress the contextual nature of mission affirm a more positive view of the world. Graham Cray, now a bishop and leader on contextualisation issues, is interested in the development of a theology of culture. He emphasises the current cultural transition from a 'modern' to 'post-modern' worldview, noting how both can be both positive and negative: 'It is not that the emerging culture is more or less friendly to the Gospel, in different ways it is both.'[66] Picking out consumerism and tribalism he outlines possible Christian responses in mission.[67] This may seem to put the emphasis on culture, but for Cray there is an unalterable core of the gospel, a 'seed' that is planted

---

[61] Ibid., 16–18.

[62] Ibid., 49–50.

[63] Ibid., 18.

[64] A much wider hint is given in Stibbe's dialogue with Moltmann, but the tendency to focus on evangelism within an evil world seems to override such hints. Mark Stibbe, 'A British Appraisal [of *Spirit of Life*]', *Journal of Pentecostal Theology* 4 (1994), 14.

[65] Nicky Gumbel, *The Heart of Revival* (Eastbourne: Kingsway, 1997), 17.

[66] Graham Cray, *From Here to Where? The Culture of the Nineties* (London: Board of Mission, 1992), 1.

[67] Graham Cray, 'New Churches for a New Millennium', *Anglicans for Renewal* 78 (1999), 16–17.

and which we need to let the Holy Spirit grow into something called the church:[68] 'The challenge to the Church is how to express the eternal truth of the Christian faith in and through this culture.'[69] There will be many forms of church in a postmodern culture: 'A plural society must have culturally plural expressions of Christian faith.'[70] Cray retains an emphasis on an unchanging gospel and on the work of the Spirit in enabling contextualisation to happen and as such he articulates a translation model of contextualisation that takes seriously study of the culture into which the church is to witness.[71] His thinking is influential in shaping fresh expressions of church within the Church of England through his chairing of a group on the 'mission-shaped church'.[72]

In a similar way Robert Warren, a charismatic leader who was the Church of England's National Officer for Evangelism, has argued that the 'first task of a missionary church is to understand the culture to which it is sent'.[73] But he goes beyond the challenge of shaping the church in response to culture: he suggests that 'the church needs to adapt both its *message* and its *way of being church* to the nature of the culture it is evangelizing'.[74] Hence Warren does not define the gospel starting from biblical texts alone, but placing them alongside an analysis of Western culture. From this he suggests that the gospel is 'that being fully human has been demonstrated for us in the person of Jesus Christ, made accessible for us through baptismal incorporation into his death, resurrection, ascension and the gift of the Holy Spirit'.[75] Warren starts by contextualising the gospel and only then does he move on to contextualise the shape of the church, and as such is more representative of a correlation approach

---

[68] Ibid., 15–16.

[69] Cray, *From Here to Where?*, 16.

[70] Ibid., 18.

[71] Cray particularly values Lamin Sanneh, *Translating the Message* (New York: Orbis, 1989).

[72] Archbishops' Council, *Mission-Shaped Church: Church Planting and Fresh Expressions of Church in a Changing Context* (London: Church House, 2004).

[73] Robert Warren, *Being Human, Being Church* (London: Marshall Pickering, 1995), 37.

[74] Ibid., 102.

[75] Ibid., 110.

to contextualisation.[76] The task of the church is both to live out this gospel and to take part in the 'moving of the Holy Spirit within our culture' to shape it in gospel ways.[77] Warren devotes much work to outlining the marks of 'missionary congregations' as he feels that lo-cal Christian communities are of vital importance in the fragmentary postmodern society of today. This approach to mission does not stress the biblical theme of the 'kingdom of God' and seems to have developed in the 1990s largely through an appreciation of the contextual mission witnessed to by Christians in other parts of the world (and of other Christian traditions) rather than relying on any earlier pentecostal theology of mission.

A significant subset of charismatic contextual approaches is those that may be termed 'Celtic'. Whilst there is debate over the histori-cal meaning and content of the term 'Celtic', authors such as Michael Mitton, Russ Parker and Ray Simpson have used it to help define their own approach to Christian life and mission. Such con-textual approaches draw not only on an analysis of present culture but also on historical (Celtic) cultures from the past. An important factor in making such ideas concrete has been the continuing development of the scattered Community of Aidan and Hilda, of which Simpson is the Guardian and prolific writer.[78] Here there is a notable emphasis on community and the church which Gavin Wakefield goes so far as to describe as *missio ecclesiae*.[79] This is proba-bly overstating the case, but a monastic model of church as 'a multi-faceted resource centre' is certainly at the heart of mission.[80] In this we may see a development of the emphasis on community seen in David Watson utilising historical more than biblical models. The 'gospel' is seen in wider terms as being 'that healing is possible for individuals, communities and creation through Christ'.[81] The

---

[76] Here I am following the categories of Peter Fulljames, *God and Creation in Intercultural Perspective* (Frankfurt: Peter Lang, 1993). For another sum-mary of approaches see Stephen B. Bevans, *Models of Contextual Theology* (New York: Orbis, 1992).

[77] Warren, *Being Human*, 50.

[78] Ray Simpson, *Exploring Celtic Spirituality: Historic Roots for Our Future* (London: Hodder & Stoughton, 1995).

[79] Wakefield, 'Mission in the Spirit', 11.

[80] Lord, 'Contextualisation in Britain', 19.

[81] Ibid., 8.

need for a holistic, incarnational, creation-affirming approach to mission is seen as key, whilst not neglecting to highlight evangelism.

The final strand of charismatic theology of mission can be termed 'catholic', picking up, perhaps unconsciously, some of the themes we saw in Gunstone. The most significant writer is Stephen Cottrell, who has been involved in promoting mission through the Springboard initiative of the Church of England, an initiative started by the Archbishops during the Decade of Evangelism. For him the key principle is that 'what we do as a church ought to arise out of what we are called to be'.[82] Starting with the church as being 'holy, catholic and apostolic' Cottrell suggests that the church is called to worship, nurture and outreach. The church *is* apostolic and hence is called to outreach/evangelism, to 'communication with the world'. Mission embraces outreach, worship and nurture and hence is defined in a broader way, although not one that immediately addresses social or ecological issues. Cottrell gives us a church-centred spirituality, yet one built upon the doctrine of incarnation, which emphasises that God is involved everywhere, in all creation. He talks of the '*everywhere*' God having to become the '*somewhere* God', although the theology underlying this is not spelt out.[83] Mission starts with a people who are 'fully Christian, fully alive' through prayer, the Eucharist and being a community together. This community shares the gospel as 'an act of service and love' rather than just a message service that encounters Christ in those outside the church as well as in the sacraments.

Summary of Themes and Concerns

We can see Anglican charismatic theology of mission as one which focuses in different ways on the blessings found in the gospel, in the kingdom, in the church community, in culture and in Christian history. Alongside these blessings is the yearning that comes from being part of the 'kingdom of darkness' yet longing for the fullness

---

[82] Stephen Cottrell, *Sacrament, Wholeness and Evangelism: A Catholic Approach* (Cambridge: Grove, 1996), 3.

[83] Ibid., 7.

of the 'kingdom of God' to be made known. The themes of gospel, evangelism, the kingdom, community, church, worship, spirituality and the world are brought together in different ways to form different theologies of mission. The theological understanding of these themes and how they interact is limited and our brief survey suggests a number of key questions that will need further exploration in developing any charismatic theology of mission. Is 'kingdom' the most important theme for mission? If so then how is it defined (narrowly in terms of evangelism or widely embracing more holistic concerns)? How important is the individual, the community and the church to mission? In what sense is the 'world' a place *of* God or *against* God? How important is history in mission?

These questions send us outwards into wider theological circles that necessitate interaction with other traditions in the theology of mission.[84] Such interaction will occupy us for much of the later part of this book, but here it is surprising that the Anglican charismatics studied show little interaction with the Anglican thinking about mission practice that has been going on at the same time. Of note here are the 'five marks of mission', a result of discussions across the Anglican Communion. These represent a holistic approach to mission which is seen as being:[85]

- to proclaim the good news of the kingdom of God.
- to teach, baptise and nurture new believers.
- to respond to human need by loving service.
- to seek to transform the unjust structures of society.
- to strive to safeguard the integrity of creation, and sustain and renew the life of the earth.

Charismatic approaches to mission in Britain have tended to stress the first three and still need a challenge to implement the last two. Recent Anglican thinking on mission believes that these 'marks'

---

[84] Robert Warren perhaps comes the closest to interacting with the wider literature, quoting Newbigin, Fung and Bosch amongst others. Yet a detailed theological interaction from an Anglican charismatic perspective is still needed.

[85] Anglican Consultative Council, 1984 and 1990. Quoted in Eleanor Johnson and John Clark (eds.), *Anglicans in Mission. A Transforming Journey; Report of MISSIO 1999* (London: SPCK, 2000), 20.

need also to take account of the 'key activity' of evangelism, to stress the contextual nature of mission, to link mission with celebration and thanksgiving and to see the church as being a people of mission.[86] These challenges are of key concern to charismatics, as we have seen, and there is therefore much that charismatics can share with the wider church on these matters.

In this chapter I have chosen to focus on Anglican charismatic thinking in Britain, influenced in part by Wimber from North America. This review has posed a number of questions that challenge the current state of mission thinking and point to the need for new ways forward. But before rushing to outline something new it is important to consider the wider pentecostal debate on mission, which covers similar ground but with greater academic rigour.

---

[86] Ibid., 19–20.

3

Pentecostal Theology of Mission

The power of God now has this city agitated as never before. Pentecost has surely come and with it the Bible evidences are following, many being converted and sanctified and filled with the Holy Ghost, speaking in tongues as they did on the day of Pentecost. The scenes that are daily enacted in the building on Azusa street and at missions and churches in other parts of the city are beyond description, and the real revival is only started, as God has been working with His children mostly, getting them through to Pentecost, and laying the foundation for a mighty wave of salvation among the unconverted.[1]

The Azusa Street Mission needs to be studied in order to rid us of our less than pristine mythologies regarding Pentecostal origins … To be sure it was charismatic … it hoped to bring an end to racism in the Church … it was committed to the idea that every member was in ministry … it was ecumenical in its character … it was evangelistic and missionary minded … it was deeply concerned with personal and social ethics … it may still hold the seeds to the continued success of the Pentecostal and Charismatic movements.[2]

At the Santa Fe Street mission in Los Angeles, 1906, a black preacher called William Seymour began to preach baptism in the Spirit and the need for speaking in tongues as the initial evidence of

---

[1] From the first edition of the Azusa Street periodical, *The Apostolic Faith* (September 1906), which heralded the key events that formed the basis of the 'Pentecostal' movement, quoted in McClung Jr, 'Try', 30–31.

[2] Cecil M. Robeck, 'Pentecostal Origins from a Global Perspective' in Hunter and Hocken (eds.), *All Together*, 180.

this baptism. When he next returned to the mission church he found the door locked against him.[3] Unfazed, he turned to a group to pray that revival might visit the town. As Easter drew near a man in the group became ill and Seymour laid on hands for healing and then for Spirit-baptism. The man was healed and 'burst forth into an unknown language' – the revival had begun. The group rushed to rent an old church on Azusa Street, described by the local paper as a 'tumble-down shack'.[4] It opened for services on Easter evening and during the next few months the crowds grew as thousands flocked to Azusa Street. Workers were organised to spread throughout the country and a vision stimulated missionaries to take 'the Azusa flame' to the ends of the earth.[5] Thus began the pentecostal and charismatic movements that were so to change the religious scene of the twentieth century.

The movement has never lacked critical debate over its theology and praxis. This began in 1906 as Seymour was visited by Charles Parham, the leader from whom he learnt his message of Spirit-baptism. Parham was not happy with the revival and gave a stinging rebuke to the church, whose response was to ask him to leave. Exactly why he was unhappy has been the subject of much debate, especially since some see Parham as the true founder of pentecostalism.[6] An aspect of this debate that is of continuing importance is the relative importance of the African-American and Western-Holiness traditions in defining the nature of pentecostalism. Despite strong arguments for the need to recapture more of the African roots of the movement, in practice the Western traditions tend to dominate the literature and so to consider academic pentecostal theology of mission is to be skewed in a particular direction. I accept this influence through this chapter, although I will be

---

[3] D. William Faupel, *The Everlasting Gospel: The Significance of Eschatology in the Development of Pentecostal Thought* (Sheffield: Sheffield Academic Press, 1996), 200.

[4] Ibid., 202.

[5] Ibid., 202, 220.

[6] James Goff sees him in this light, *Fields White Unto Harvest: Charles F. Parham and the Missionary Origins of Pentecostalism* (Fayetteville: University of Arkansas Press, 1988). Most scholars remain unconvinced and focus more on Seymour. For more on this debate see Faupel, *Everlasting Gospel*, 206–12; Hollenweger, *Pentecostalism*, 20–24.

taking things in a more contextual African-informed direction subsequently. Despite the differing convictions, there is a widely shared
desire to recapture some of the theological and practical threads that
were glimpsed during the first ten years of the pentecostal movement.[7] Drawing on this desire I want to suggest in this chapter that
pentecostal theology of mission has focused on particular blessings
that arise out of Christology, pneumatology and eschatology, a
threefold pattern evident in the start of the movement. In more recent years questions regarding the holistic nature of mission and the
importance of ecclesiology have forced pentecostals to expand their
theology of mission to embrace a wider sphere of blessing. In the
following sections I want to give more detail to this thinking as it has
developed before asking what are the challenges such an understanding of mission faces.

Early Pentecostal Theology of Mission

We can see early pentecostal theology of mission as one that embraced a fivefold blessing of Christ witnessed to by the Bible and
shared in evangelism. The task of evangelism is blessed through the
revelation and power of the Holy Spirit that marks the inauguration
of God's kingdom. Blessings will be completed when Christ returns, which is expected soon. Looking at this in more detail we
note that the original gospel message that was proclaimed was diverse in content, but many scholars follow the five doctrines
identified by Donald Dayton: justification, sanctification, healing,
the pre-millennial return of Christ and baptism of the Holy Spirit.[8]
These all show a distinctly Christological orientation to the pentecostal message: the work of Christ on the cross assured justification,
sanctification and healing; the ascended Christ baptised the believer
with the Holy Spirit; the returning Christ was the ultimate hope of
the believer's destiny.[9] The basis for this outlook was a conservative
approach to the Bible. Pentecostals were characterised as 'people of

---

[7] E.g. Steven J. Land, *Pentecostal Spirituality: A Passion for the Kingdom*
(Sheffield: Sheffield Academic Press, 1993), 47.
[8] Dayton, *Theological Roots*, 19–21; Faupel, *Everlasting Gospel*, 28.
[9] Faupel, *Everlasting Gospel*, 30.

the Book' with a desire to bring word and Spirit, exegesis and experience, together. The outworking of this Christology is seen primarily through the mission imperative to evangelism. They saw the Bible as commanding the proclamation of the gospel to the ends of the earth and that is what they tried to do. This focus on evangelism was also characteristic of the existing Holiness and missionary movements that fed the pentecostal movement, if taken by pentecostals in a more eschatological and experiential direction. Pentecostal theology of mission presupposes a conservative approach to the Bible that demands the proclamation of a Christological gospel to the world that the 'lost' may be 'saved'.

The pentecostal movement has a natural emphasis on the Holy Spirit understood as essentially the *missionary Spirit*. It is the Spirit that empowers and sends Christian disciples in mission and this is what the early history of the pentecostal movement testifies to.[10] This understanding is based on a Lukan pneumatology that is seen to be thoroughly oriented towards mission, as John Penney has recently argued in detail against a number of critiques.[11] Here we have a classical understanding of *missio Dei* focused on the Spirit.[12] It is an experience of God the Holy Spirit that empowers and sends disciples out in mission and Pentecost is the prototype: a 'baptism in the Spirit' that generates mission. Steven Land speaks of an 'experiential primitivism' that characterises pentecostals – there is a desire to return to the primitive experience of Pentecost and through this become a community of mission.[13] The experience of the Spirit is seen in specific 'crisis points' to which testimony is made as a part of mission. Thus the Holy Spirit is linked to experience in a personal rather than a general way, and it is through these specific experiences that God motivates mission.

Considering these experiences in more detail, what they represent for pentecostals is an experience of the 'revelation' and 'power' of the transcendent God. The gift of tongues was particularly important in the early years of the pentecostal movement: as evidence

---

[10] Ibid., 214–26.

[11] John Michael Penney, *The Missionary Emphasis of Lukan Pneumatology* (Sheffield: Sheffield Academic Press, 1997).

[12] Bosch, *Transforming Mission*, 389–93; Pomerville, *Third Force*, 137–43.

[13] Land, *Pentecostal Spirituality*, 60–61.

of having received the 'baptism in the Spirit' and as languages for evangelising the world. The latter was a significant encouragement to world mission although, as Gary McGee concludes, the evidence that pentecostals did in fact preach in new languages proved very difficult to establish.[14] As a result, McGee suggests that as early as 1907 there was a shift towards emphasising general experiences of 'signs and wonders' which would accompany evangelism, rather than tongues in particular. McGee sees pentecostal mission as uniquely characterised by the development of a *'radical strategy* – an apocalyptic scenario of divine intervention in signs and wonders to ensure that every tribe and nation would hear the gospel before the close of human history'.[15] This 'divine intervention' was not without opposition, and Pomerville suggests that pentecostals viewed 'these times clearly as days of power-encounter where the forces of God clash with the forces of evil in cosmic struggle'.[16]

Thus an understanding of the Spirit is linked to eschatology, which is also central to pentecostal theology of mission and indeed to the later charismatic theology of mission, as we have seen. For pentecostals history will reach its climax when Jesus returns and the eschatological kingdom will be established. Eschatology for pentecostals focuses on two particular beliefs: the eschatological kingdom has been inaugurated in the Holy Spirit; and Jesus is returning soon. Pentecost is seen against the eschatological hope of Israel, and Peter's use of the quotation from Joel is significant (Acts 2:17–21). Pentecost represented the time of eschatological fulfilment that inaugurated the kingdom which is characterised by the Spirit and which implies that now is the time of world mission.[17] The 'signs and wonders', and indeed all gifts of the Spirit, are 'eschatological, proleptic signs of a kingdom of joy where sorrow, death and sin are

---

[14]   Gary B. McGee, '"Power from on High": A Historical Perspective on the Radical Strategy in Missions' in Wonsuk Ma and Robert P. Menzies (eds.), *Pentecostalism in Context: Essays in Honor of William W. Menzies* (Sheffield: Sheffield Academic Press, 1997), 327–8; Faupel, *Everlasting Gospel*, 220, 228.

[15]   McGee, 'Power', 322.

[16]   Pomerville, *Third Force*, 57. Such an outlook continues, as evidenced in the later charismatic movement, Wimber and Springer, *Power Evangelism* (1992), 28–33.

[17]   Penney, *Missionary Emphasis*, 84–90.

put down and banished'.[18] Pentecostals picked up the existing expectation of the imminent pre-millennial return of Christ and felt that his return was nearer because of the 'signs and wonders'. Using a 'latter rain' motif from Joel, early pentecostals understood the end of the age as marked by 'God's sovereign acts' in the same way as at the start of the age (the church of Acts).[19] At the same time they believed that 'history was getting darker and God would ultimately need to impose his will from outside the historical process'.[20] The second coming of Christ would therefore be a time of judgment on the world as well as a blessing for those belonging to Christ. This gave a great urgency to evangelism: to rescue the 'lost' from the darkness of the world before Christ came in judgment.

The Search for a Holistic Pentecostal Theology of Mission

As noted in the Introduction, the last twenty years have seen a yearning within the pentecostal community for a more holistic approach to mission, one that embraces more of the world within the blessings of God by the Spirit. This has been stimulated by the critique that pentecostals are only interested in evangelism and steer away from social and political issues.[21] McClung argues that more holistic approaches are needed to face the challenges of the twenty-first century with its 'out-of-control global changes'.[22] McClung proposes a pentecostal missiological paradigm based on the centrality of word (exegesis) and Spirit (experience). From this 'internal soul of Pentecostalism' there is a reaching outwards in four directions: eschatology, an expectation of Christ's return; evangelism, which is prioritised; ecology, that includes 'prophetic social activism'; and ecumenism, meaning co-operation in mission.

---

[18] Land, *Pentecostal Spirituality*, 177.

[19] Faupel, *Everlasting Gospel*, 30–34.

[20] Ibid., 75.

[21] The various criticisms are usefully summarised by Veli-Matti Kärkkäinen, '"Truth on Fire": Pentecostal Theology of Mission and the Challenges of a New Millennium', *Asian Journal of Pentecostal Studies* 3.1 (2000), 46–9.

[22] McClung Jr, 'Try', 46.

McClung concludes by emphasising that his paradigm is held together by the central Christological confession identified by Dayton worked out through evangelism by '"Great Commission" Christians'. This proposal gives a more holistic understanding of mission, although it is not clear how the Christ–evangelism 'focus' relates to the word–Spirit 'internal soul' within the missiology. Presumably both are to be held together, although no theological framework is presented that embraces both. It appears that McClung is wanting to stress the themes of Christ, evangelism, the Scriptures, the Holy Spirit and eschatology which are central to pentecostal theology of mission as we have seen. To these he adds ecumenism and ecology, but their addition seems more pragmatic than theological. There is a need to present a pentecostal theological understanding of mission that is more holistic. McGee identifies the two crucial issues of ecumenism and social action and develops a more integrated approach than McClung by linking these to the gifts of the Holy Spirit. He links ecumenism with the work of the Holy Spirit in granting gifts to non-pentecostal Christians. Allan Anderson suggests a more holistic approach to mission on the basis that one of the results of the experience of the Spirit is a 'pentecostal theology of liberation'.[23] This liberation is holistic and not just confined to the 'spiritual' sphere but has to do 'with dignity, authority and power over all types of oppression'.[24] This seeking after liberation has, he suggests, always been a part of pentecostal practice but is often overlooked. These are significant suggestions that indicate the possibilities of a holistic pentecostal theology of mission based on a broader pneumatology.

Amos Yong proposes a different and provocative broadening of pneumatology in order to address the issue of 'other religions' in the mission of the church. His basic argument is that Christology as a basis for inter-religious interactions has come to an impasse. What is needed is to develop pneumatological approaches using the insights from a pentecostal-charismatic perspective. An understanding of 'Spirit' is explored to find some common ground between different religions. He argues that 'the Holy Spirit is both present and at work in the non-Christian faiths' but discernment is key – not everything is of the Holy Spirit. Yong's work focuses on this theme of discern-

[23]   Anderson, *Pentecostalism*, 261.
[24]   Ibid., 269.

ment but he does offer suggestions as to how this outlook could affect mission: 'Focus would not lie as much on conversion across religious lines – thus confirming the dualism between Church and world, culture and other faith traditions – as on transfiguration of the non-Christian faiths from within via the germination of the Gospel seed through the power of the Spirit.'[25] We will consider Yong's ideas more fully in Chapter 6.

Various other scholars prefer to stress a broader understanding of the eschatological kingdom. The significant collection of essays entitled *Called and Empowered* stresses the importance of 'kingdom' in a pentecostal understanding of global mission. This theme has been pioneered by Gordon Fee, the pentecostal New Testament scholar. He has united the traditional pentecostal stress on the 'futuristic nature of the kingdom of God' with an 'emphasis on the present power of the kingdom'.[26] Murray Dempster argues that Pentecost and the kingdom are linked in Luke's theology of church mission: 'to be committed to the Holy Spirit's work at Pentecost entails the antecedent commitment to Jesus' work in inaugurating the kingdom'.[27] This kingdom provides the integrating theme for the church's ministries of evangelism and social concern. Dempster talks of 'proclaiming the kingdom in spoken word', 'picturing the kingdom in a social witness' and 'manifesting the kingdom in moral deeds'. He explains these in terms of evangelism, *koinonia* (fellowship) and social concern – a theology of the kingdom as seen through its outworkings in the holistic ministry of the church. Douglas Petersen goes further in stressing the importance of context to an understanding of the biblical kingdom. He proposes a revised liberationist hermeneutical cycle in which 'our interpretation of the Bible ... is dictated by the continuing changes in our present-day reality'.[28] Using an example from Latin America, he starts with the

---

[25] Yong, *Discerning*, 63.

[26] Murray W. Dempster, Byron D. Klaus and Douglas Petersen (eds.), *Called and Empowered: Global Mission in Pentecostal Perspective* (Sheffield: Sheffield Academic Press, 1991), 3–4.

[27] Murray W. Dempster, 'Evangelism, Social Concern and the Kingdom of God' in Dempster, Klaus and Petersen (eds.), *Called and Empowered*, 23.

[28] Douglas Petersen, 'The Kingdom of God and the Hermeneutical Circle: Pentecostal Praxis in the Third World' in Dempster, Klaus and Petersen (eds.), *Called and Empowered*, 45. For a more detailed exposition see Petersen, *Not by Might*.

plight of children, which is then analysed to identify a variety of factors that cause their suffering. Then Petersen moves to 'reflection on the revealed word of God' centred around the theme of the kingdom. This then leads to practical action, which the organisation he leads has seen to be successful.

The Church and Mission

Despite the broadening of the scope of mission, the mediation of God's blessing is still often seen in a very individualistic way. Within the last ten years some pentecostal scholars have attempted to correct this through a greater appreciation of ecclesiology, the community as the place of God's blessing. In the early years an ecclesiastical primitivism and the urgency of the 'radical mission' task meant that institutional matters were left aside until it became clearer that Christ had delayed his return.[29] There was a focus on individual believers being led by the Spirit in mission. However, the sense of community was never absent: the Spirit came upon all believers equipping them as a whole for missionary witness. The vital importance of lay ministry in pentecostal mission is often commented on – 'all in the body of Christ are ministers and everyone a preacher'.[30] A background assumption here is that the Holy Spirit is primarily, or even exclusively, seen as operating within the believing church communities. In mission the Spirit leads in evangelism which results in the creation of new believing communities. Pentecostalism has grown in many parts of the world through church planting that accompanies an evangelistic emphasis. This leads McClung to emphasise the importance of the 'Church Growth Movement' for pentecostal theology of mission and Pomerville to emphasise 'Great Commission mission'.[31]

Summarising pentecostal ecclesiology, Peter Hocken suggests that pentecostals 'commonly believe that the one church of Christ is

---

[29] Land, *Pentecostal Spirituality*, 60; McGee, 'Power', 335.

[30] L. Grant McClung Jr, 'Missiology' in S.M. Burgess, G.B. McGee and P.H. Alexander (eds.), *Dictionary of Pentecostal and Charismatic Movements* (Grand Rapids: Regency Reference Library, 1988), 608.

[31] McClung Jr, 'Try', 43; Pomerville, *Third Force*, 143.

composed of all who are regenerate in Jesus through repentance and faith … While pentecostals have nearly always affirmed the invisibility of the universal church, they have regularly used the term *assembly* for the visible local congregation.'[32] Hocken suggests that the main pentecostal contribution to ecclesiology is found in the 'charismatic endowments of the Holy Spirit … as forming and shaping the church' and in the focus on building up indigenous churches.[33] Restorationist charismatic approaches have been shaped by David Lille, who brought many ideas from his Plymouth Brethren background. Central to this is an emphasis on the priesthood of all believers and the charismatic equipping of church members. Also, 'each local church is a full manifestation of the church' and together this stresses the blessings that God grants by the Spirit to Christian communities wherever they are.[34] However, I want to suggest that pentecostal ecclesiology has stressed either the universal or the particular nature of the church but has not been so good at connecting the two. The universal church is seen in 'invisible' spiritual terms rather than in 'visible' denominational terms, which allows us to appreciate the Spirit's work across denominations, 'drawing all together in one bond of love, one church, one body of Christ'.[35] But there is a need to overcome the reluctance to speak of 'visible embodiments of the universal church' – we can be left with an ideal still waiting to be made more concrete.

As regards forming indigenous churches, it was a 'high-church' Anglican missionary, Roland Allen, whose ideas crucially influenced pentecostal approaches to indigenisation.[36] His emphasis on the work of the Spirit in Acts combined with a stress on Pauline methods of church planting were attractive to pentecostals. His ideas were developed by Melvin Hodges, an Assemblies of God

---

[32] P.D. Hocken, 'Church, Theology of the' in Burgess and van der Maas (eds.), *Dictionary of Pentecostal and Charismatic Movements*, 544.

[33] Ibid., 547.

[34] Ibid., 550.

[35] *The Apostolic Faith*, quoted in ibid., 545.

[36] Gary B. McGee, 'Missions, Overseas (North American)' in Burgess, McGee and Alexander (eds.), *Dictionary of Pentecostal and Charismatic Movements*, 621.

missionary, in his highly influential book *The Indigenous Church*, originally published in 1953.[37] Hodges combines some insights from Allen with the 'three-self' policy of Rufus Anderson and Henry Venn. For Hodges there are three basic elements which made the church indigenous: self-propagation, self-support and self-government. Allan Anderson suggests that this 'three-self' policy was 'automatically and effortlessly achieved by many Pentecostal movements before this goal was realised by older western mission churches'.[38] However, he also critiques Hodges for not recognising that the 'three-selfs' will not lead to indigenous churches unless 'those churches are grounded in the thought patterns and symbolism of popular culture'. Also, Hodges does not take account of the pentecostal 'indigenous churches' established without the help of any 'foreign missionaries'. The pentecostal emphasis on indigenous churches is under threat because present-day globalisation means that pentecostal missionaries are tempted to carry a 'transnational' mentality, according to Anderson.[39] A recent collection of articles on pentecostal mission is entitled *The Globalization of Pentecostalism* and talks of a pentecostal 'global culture'.[40] There appears a temptation for Western pentecostals to talk of 'globalisation' and non-Western pentecostals to talk of 'indigenisation'.

Pentecostal ecclesiology has developed through a missionary, evangelistic praxis rather than through sustained theological reflection. However, more recently there has been great reflection motivated by a number of themes. Land talks of a 'missionary fellowship' as the setting for his exploration of pentecostal spirituality. For him the church is an 'eschatological trinitarian fellowship' within which the 'Pentecostal passion for the kingdom of God is formed and expressed'.[41] The church is 'a church on the way to the

---

[37] Melvin L. Hodges, *The Indigenous Church* (Springfield: Gospel, 1976), 22.

[38] Allan Anderson, 'The Gospel and Culture in Pentecostal Mission in the Third World', *Missionalia* 27.2 (1999), 223–4.

[39] Allan Anderson, 'Global Pentecostalism in the New Millennium' in Allan H. Anderson and Walter J. Hollenweger (eds.), *Pentecostals After a Century: Global Perspectives on a Movement in Transition* (Sheffield: Sheffield Academic Press, 1999), 218–19.

[40] Dempster, Klaus and Petersen (eds.), *Globalization of Pentecostalism*, xiii.

[41] Land, *Pentecostal Spirituality*, 178, 205.

kingdom ... a movement of the Spirit' more than an institution.[42] Simon Chan argues that pentecostals have tended to see the church in purely sociological terms – a reality largely dependent on the actions of its members. In contrast he argues that the church 'is a spiritual reality that exists prior to the individual Christians – prior to the foundation of the world'.[43] He sees a need to counteract individualism and a focus on human rather than divine action. Chan proposes three key characteristics of the church: as a catholic community, a healing community and a truth-traditioning community. On the one hand he is concerned to broaden the pentecostal understanding of the church, although in doing so he seems largely to ignore the missionary nature of the church that is central to pentecostal ecclesiology. Admittedly Chan's concern is the passing on of 'tradition' but his approach shows a pentecostal temptation to develop ecclesiology in isolation from wider society.

Pentecostal Theology of Mission and Lausanne II

The recent developments in pentecostal theology of mission can be seen to draw heavily on the consensus and tensions evident in the Lausanne II world mission conference of 1989. It will be useful to outline some of this background in order to put such theology in a broader context. The two Lausanne conferences represented a chance for evangelical mission leaders to come together for inspiration and to work towards consensus.[44] Although perhaps Lausanne II tended towards inspiration rather than listening and consensus-building it does represent an important point in evangelical and pentecostal mission thinking. Building on Lausanne I, convened by Billy Graham in 1974, this new conference took as its theme to 'Proclaim Christ until he comes: calling the whole church to take the whole gospel to the whole world.'[45]

---

[42] Ibid., 178.

[43] Simon Chan, *Pentecostal Theology and the Christian Spiritual Tradition* (Sheffield: Sheffield Academic Press, 2000), 97.

[44] There is always a tension between these two aims in any mission conference, Norman E. Thomas, 'World Mission Conferences: What Impact do they Have?', *International Bulletin of Missionary Research* 20 (1996), 151.

[45] J.D. Douglas (ed.), *Proclaim Christ until He Comes* (Minneapolis: World Wide, 1989).

Lausanne I saw a 'quarantine regarding charismatics' which was overturned in Lausanne II where the opening address called for evangelicals and charismatics to come together in 'a new ... partnership in world evangelization'.[46] An evening was given over to consider 'The power and work of the Holy Spirit' to which Jim Packer and Jack Hayford spoke from evangelical and charismatic perspectives respectively. Packer highlighted what he saw as the main problem of today, that 'people are being promised an experience of the Spirit in situations where far too little is being said about Christ'.[47] He spent most of his address expounding 'the work of the Holy Spirit in the experienced event of personal conviction and conversion'. Jack Hayford opened his address with the words, 'In discussing the power of the Holy Spirit in evangelism, we are at the cutting edge of the miraculous.'[48] But he was keen to build up a holistic understanding of the Spirit's work in spreading the gospel and emphasise Jesus: 'The world needs Jesus – in all his *saving* power, in all his *healing* power, in all his *delivering* power.'[49] Hayford stressed the need all Christians have for the *fullness* of the Spirit as the theme that unites evangelicals and pentecostals. It appears clear that Hayford went to greater lengths than Packer to bridge the divisions, and as Coote comments afterwards, 'Several of my fellow participants agreed that the biblical support and the pastoral, personalized approach that Hayford employed carried the evening.'[50] However, this positive evaluation covers over the cracks and James Scherer suggests that 'many delegates at Manila were offended by the charismatic manifestations'.[51] Reflecting later, John Stott wondered if a

---

[46] Coote, 'Lausanne II', 13; Ibid., 50.

[47] Douglas (ed.), *Proclaim Christ*, 100.

[48] Ibid., 108.

[49] Ibid., 113.

[50] Coote, 'Lausanne II', 13. This comment is also backed up by Nichols, who says that 'The session was generally welcomed by the audience ... There was a sense of maturity about this balance, and a sense of relaxation that even the Lausanne Movement was able to let the program go free to experience a touch of Charismatic worship.' Alan Nichols (ed.), *The Whole Gospel for the Whole World: Story of Lausanne II Congress on World Evangelization* (Ventura: LCWE & Regal, 1989), 55.

[51] Alan Neely and James A. Scherer, 'San Antonio and Manila 1989: " ... Like Ships in the Night?"', *Missiology* 18.2 (1990), 144.

debate rather than presentations might have been better, picking up on the Lausanne Oslo consultation in 1985 on the work of the Holy Spirit.[52] The 'Manila Manifesto' which resulted from Lausanne II speaks of the holistic work of the Spirit in evangelism:

> It is he who anoints the messenger, confirms the Word, prepares the hearer, convicts the sinful, enlightens the blind, gives life to the dead, enables us to repent and believe, unites us to the body of Christ, assures us that we are God's children, leads us into Christ-like character and service, and sends us out in our turn to be Christ's witnesses.[53]

This fits with the evangelism-focused, Christologically inspired understanding of the Spirit we found in pentecostal theology of mission, but notably ignores the issue of 'signs and wonders' by which the power and revelation of God are received. Here perhaps is the heart of evangelical–pentecostal divisions in understanding the work of the Spirit in mission.

This focus on evangelism lies in tension with a desire for more holistic understandings of mission. The setting of Lausanne II in Manila highlighted the link between evangelism and social action with the President of the Philippines addressing the conference and challenging people to follow Jesus in addressing issues of poverty and injustice. Lausanne I had expressed 'penitence both for our neglect and for having sometimes regarded evangelism and social action as mutually exclusive … we affirm that evangelism and socio-political involvement are both part of our Christian duty'.[54]

Yet the debate continued with a number of leaders arguing that in practice social responsibility was being downplayed.[55] This led to a consultation in 1982 in which a threefold relationship between evangelism and social activity was agreed on, representing

---

[52] John Stott, 'Twenty Years after Lausanne: Some Personal Reflections', *International Bulletin of Missionary Research* 19.2 (1995), 52. Oslo is mentioned by Stott and also Nichols (ed.), *The Whole Gospel*, 53.

[53] Douglas (ed.), *Proclaim Christ*, 31.

[54] Ibid., 21.

[55] Timothy Chester, *Awakening to a World of Need: The Recovery of Evangelical Social Concern* (Leicester: Inter-Varsity Press, 1993), 83–8.

the consensus reached prior to Lausanne II: social activity is a *consequence* of evangelism, a *bridge* to evangelism and a *partner* of evangelism.[56]

Lausanne II represented in many ways an exposition of this consensus given from different perspectives. Tom Houston spoke of how as 'evangelism and social concern were inseparable in the mind of Jesus, they must be inseparable in our minds and ministry'.[57] Vinay Samuel articulated what he saw as a crucial assumption, that 'the faithfulness to the gospel includes a call to respond to the needs of the whole person and to all human needs'.[58] Caesar Molebatsi challenged delegates to see that it 'is the job of the evangelist and the missionary to address all forms of oppression' and that for all evangelicals 'Our cry is a political cry: the proclamation of a new King!'[59] Yet a tension still remained that is seen in a number of the concluding addresses, which seem to revert to an emphasis on evangelism. Luis Palau stated that 'evangelism is the best form of social action … because evangelism deals with the root of the problem, not with the symptoms'.[60] Thomas Wang stated that 'When individuals are transformed [after conviction by the gospel], society is transformed.' There was a renewed emphasis on the Great Commission understood in terms of evangelism and supported by statistics on the number of 'Great Commission Christians'.[61] This tension between evangelism and social action has continued in evangelical and pentecostal mission thinking, as we have seen. There is a need to develop a shared theological basis that might bring these concerns together in a more unified way.

There were hopes that Lausanne II might tackle in more detail the question of how indigenous churches could be developed. Lausanne I admitted that 'Missions have all too frequently exported with the gospel an alien culture.'[62] Following on from this, a consul-

---

[56] Stott, 'Twenty Years', 52.

[57] Douglas (ed.), *Proclaim Christ*, 156.

[58] Ibid., 289.

[59] Ibid., 296.

[60] Ibid., 369.

[61] Ibid., 353.

[62] Ibid., 22. Efiong Utuk commented that Lausanne 'directly acknowledged the inevitability of cultural pluralism and debunked the old position which clearly ties Christianity primarily to Western culture'. Efiong S.

tation on 'Gospel and Culture' was held in 1978 in Willowbank that generally opted for a 'dynamic equivalence' model for bringing together 'gospel' and 'culture'.[63] This emphasises the need to translate the 'gospel' (which is given by God) into different cultures.[64] At Willowbank it was recognised that further thinking was needed on this issue by evangelicals and hence expected that some of the issues would be picked up at Lausanne II.[65] However, once again Lausanne II seems to be caught in a tension. The opening and closing addresses focus on culture only in terms of the 'need to take the gospel cross-culturally to those groups of unreached people who have never had an adequate internal witness'.[66] There is a need for 'costly identification [that] means learning another language, adjusting to their customs and lifestyles'.[67] But the focus is on a 'pure', 'undiluted gospel of Jesus Christ' which is shared across cultures that sadly exist only 'As the result of God's punishment for the pride of mankind at Babel'.[68] This 'gospel-positive culture-negative' approach contrasts with some of the deeper discussions in the track on 'cross-cultural mission'. In these discussions more positive evaluations of Buddhist and Muslim cultures and religions were explored.[69] The conclusion reached was that:

---

[62] (*Continued*) Utuk, 'From Wheaton to Lausanne: The Road to Modification of Contemporary Evangelical Mission Theology', *Missiology* 14.2 (1986), 214.

[63] For the wider debate under the title of 'contextualisation', see Bosch, *Transforming Mission*, 421ff.

[64] The evangelical debate on this issue can be traced back to the 'three-selfs' formulated by Rufus Anderson and Henry Venn (General Secretary of the evangelical Church Missionary Society) during the last century. Indigenous churches were to be self-governing, self-supporting and self-propagating. These principles and their outworkings have been criticised (e.g. Bosch, *Transforming Mission*, 450) but represent a cultural challenge to those involved in mission.

[65] Stott, 'Twenty Years', 50.

[66] Douglas (ed.), *Proclaim Christ*, 60.

[67] Ibid., 375.

[68] Ibid., 354, 171.

[69] On Buddhism see Douglas (ed.), *Proclaim Christ*, 441; J.R. Davis, *Poles Apart* (Bangalore: ATA, 1993). On Islam see Phil Parshall, *New Paths in Muslim Evangelism: Evangelical Approaches to Contextualization* (Grand Rapids: Baker, 1980).

The receiving cultures must have freedom under Christ and, in light of the Scriptures, develop a Christian faith which has the same effect on their culture as Jesus Christ had on his ... Every Christian community must be aware of the possibility of slipping into undesirable syncretism as they flesh out the gospel in the particular local context. Yet, unless the churches deliberately contextualize the gospel in their cultures, the church remains a foreign institution and evangelism is throttled.[70]

Given the underlying tensions at Lausanne II it is not surprising to find little but a general statement in its final report: 'The balance between gospel and context must be carefully maintained. We must understand the context in order to address it, but the context must not be allowed to distort the gospel.'[71]

From our perspective it is interesting to note how the tensions evident at Lausanne II in understanding the work of the Holy Spirit in mission, in searching for a holistic approach to mission and in understanding contextualisation are also evident in the pentecostal and charismatic theologies of mission we have been outlining. This is suggestive of the continuing need to develop an underlying theological basis from which some of these tensions can be better resolved. This book begins such a development by setting off from a charismatic rather than an evangelical starting point, allowing for the obvious overlap in these terms. In the wider mission thinking this may enable us to trace an alternative route to that taken by evangelicals since Lausanne II.

Summary of Themes

We have seen that pentecostal theology of mission has as its essential pattern particular understandings of Christology, pneumatology and eschatology. These understandings have been seen as limited in the face of various pressures. Broadly speaking, we can say that pentecostal theologians have held to the original Christology and broadened their understanding of either pneumatology or eschatology in order to address issues of holistic mission, other faiths and the

---

[70] Douglas (ed.), *Proclaim Christ*, 389–90.

[71] Ibid., 35.

church. The appeal to a broader eschatology focused on the present nature of the kingdom seems the best way forward in understanding holistic mission. A broader pneumatology can help deepen understandings of the church, issues of indigenisation and issues of 'religious experience' particularly as they relate to other faiths. Based on this analysis I want to suggest that in moving on from here any pentecostal theology of mission needs to address five key themes: holistic mission, experience, context, community and spirituality.

It is worth considering how the metaphors of blessing and yearning might contribute to these five before we examine them in detail. Holistic mission flows from the blessings of the eschatological kingdom that has been already inaugurated. It is a kingdom filled with the blessings of liberation, mercy, care, justice, reconciliation and healing. Yet it is a kingdom that is still yearned for as we await Jesus' coming again. We live in the 'not yet' of exile when creation groans and our healing is not complete. Christian experience in mission is filled with the blessings of meeting Christ, seeing the joy of restored relationships with God, of 'new creations', of people justified and sanctified. It is an experience of the 'annunciations' and the richness, the fullness, the 'baptism' of the Holy Spirit. Experiences of the Spirit bring revelation, power, fruit and passion for the Bible. Yet this experience is incomplete – we experience also our sin and lostness, heartwrung sighs of sorrow over what has not yet come. We yearn for others in their lostness, reaching out in prayer, longing that others may meet with Christ. The blessings we experience are appropriate to our particular context and are 'indigenous' to us. Blessings of music, art and worship raise us towards God and we discover the blessings of God in all things, even within the experience of those outside the Christian faith. God's blessing knows no limits and always seeks to meet people where they are. Yet many people are far from God and yearn for deep blessings that meet them where they are and bring them fulfilment. Others in contexts of pain and suffering long for God to lead them out into a spacious place of refreshment. Blessings are not just individual but communal, bringing groups of people alive in the Spirit. Renewal brings the blessings of sharing and generosity, of praise and goodwill, of partnership and growth. Yet even when renewal sweeps the church and it becomes enlivened and outward directed, there is still a sense of the current low-level of church life, of blessings yet to be experienced. We mourn over the state of our churches and yearn for something better, a reviving of what seems downfallen. In all things we live a life of blessing and yearning, a spirituality that needs developing if we are to drink more deeply of God's motivation for mission. Mission is not something we *ought* to do, but something that cannot but spring from the well of blessing and yearning. A spirituality of yearning intercession and inbreaking spiritual gifts, of learning to wait on the Father's voice and also to move in his power, of longing for the world to change and finding ourselves sent in weakness to bring about that change. Such is the profound picture of mission offered from the Father by the Spirit in Christ. It is within this rich cross-over of theme and metaphor that this work on the theology of mission is set.

Part 2

A Charismatic
Theology of Mission

4

Holistic Mission

To my friends and teacher in the Pentecostal Movement who taught me to love the Bible and to my teachers and friends in the Presbyterian Church who taught me to understand it. To my friends and scholars in the Pentecostal Movement who taught me to criticize and understand Pentecostalism's weaknesses and blind spots and to the friends and scholars in the universal Church who showed me Pentecostalism's strengths and potentials.[1]

There is 'a larger problem, namely, the lack of awareness of being a part of the larger Christian tradition … what Pentecostals need is to discover the deeper roots of their faith and experience. There is much in the contemplative tradition which resonates with Pentecostalism which Pentecostals need to explore further.'[2]

Sitting in one of those uncomfortable university chairs I found myself arguing a proposal for research in charismatic theology of mission. 'Why pentecostalism? Why the charismatic movement?' I was asked. 'They have been the source of so many bad things.' Those outside the movement can seem to speak a different language and are not always eager to learn from us. Yet many within the movement look outwards: as one friend said recently, 'I have left the triumphalism behind but want to keep hold of the good – how do we do it?' This is a journey many have undertaken, as Walter Hollenweger's dedication above illustrates. Somehow we are to hold to the essentials and yet be ready to be stretched to embrace

---

[1] Hollenweger, *Pentecostalism*, dedication.
[2] Chan, *Pentecostal Theology*, 11.

what the universal church has to teach us. For Hollenweger that was to do with biblical and critical learning; for Simon Chan it was the contemplative tradition; for us here it is the wider thinking on eschatology and mission. How can we keep the urgency and passion for mission, especially evangelism, yet broaden our understanding and allow the Spirit to bring truth from unexpected places to bear on our situation? This is what we begin to explore in this chapter.

Eschatology and Mission

I have suggested that eschatology forms one of the central themes of charismatic theology of mission. Such theology focuses on the inauguration of the kingdom of God by the Spirit and a belief in the imminent return of Jesus. Together these understandings give a natural focus on evangelism, the desire to see people respond to Christ and enter the kingdom before Christ comes again. However, it does provide problems when attempting a more holistic understanding of mission and I want to suggest that we need to re-consider our understanding of eschatology in order to embrace a wider appreciation of the blessings of mission. My motivation is similar to that of Peter Althouse in his recent study of pentecostal eschatology, although here I want to approach the subject starting with the theology of mission.[3] Although the rediscovery of eschatology was one of the dominant themes in theology of the twentieth century it is still the case that, as David Bosch put it, 'In every Christian tradition and in every continent we are still in the midst of a movement to reformulate a theology of mission in the light of an authentic eschatology.'[4] This is also surprising from a pentecostal perspective as eschatology is seen as the 'mother of pentecostal missiology'.[5] Althouse explores how four pentecostal thinkers have re-visioned early pentecostal eschatology, although there still appears a reluctance to apply these insights in the wider literature on mission. Perhaps there is a certain

---

[3] Peter Althouse, *Spirit of the Last Days* (London: T&T Clark, 2003).

[4] Bosch, *Transforming Mission*, 508.

[5] V.M. Kärkkäinen, 'Missiology: Pentecostal and Charismatic' in Burgess and van der Maas (eds.), *Dictionary of Pentecostal and Charismatic Movements*, 879, quoting D. William Faupel.

resistance to challenge and develop a different approach to eschatology in the fear of losing what has already been gained.

Bosch suggests that there were four major 'eschatological schools' in German Protestantism that had a significant impact on twentieth-century theology. First, he suggests that Karl Barth is representative of approaches that stress 'the absolute transcendence of God and his being totally separate from the world'.[6] Secondly, Rudolf Bultmann is representative of approaches that are more individualistic and interior, seeing 'eschatology as the even which unfolds itself between the proclaimed word ... and the individual human being'.[7] Thirdly, Althaus and C.H. Dodd are representative of approaches that see the kingdom 'actualised' and present today, if yet hidden, thus playing down the future element of eschatology.[8] Finally, there is the 'salvation-historical' school which in mission circles was very significant at the 1952 International Missionary Council conference at Willingen. This conference was in part motivated to consider eschatology because of the 'missionaries expelled from that "jewel" of missions – China'.[9] The most influential speakers at this conference were Oscar Cullmann, Walter Freytag and Hans Margull. Cullmann argued powerfully that 'the reality of external historical events is central to salvation-history' and that 'The missionary work of the Church is the eschatological foretaste of the kingdom of God, and the biblical hope of the "end" constitutes the keenest incentive to action.'[10] Freytag argued that biblical sending is linked with eschatological hope with now being 'salvation-time' when we are sent to proclaim the gospel, carrying on until the 'end-time' when the end will come.[11] Margull wanted to extend mission beyond proclamation of the gospel to be rather an

---

[6] Bosch, *Transforming Mission*, 502.

[7] Ibid.

[8] Ibid., 503.

[9] Norman E. Thomas (ed.), *Readings in World Mission* (London: SPCK, 1995), 305.

[10] Gerald G. O'Collins, 'Salvation' in D.N. Freedman (ed.), *Anchor Bible Dictionary* (New York: Doubleday, 1992), 913; Oscar Cullmann, 'Mission in God's Eschatology' in Norman E. Thomas (ed.), *Readings in World Mission* (London: SPCK, 1995), 307.

[11] Walter Freytag, 'Mission in View of the End' in Thomas (ed.), *Readings*, 310.

'eschatological ministry as we participate in Christ's ministry'.[12] These themes from the 'salvation-historical' school have in many ways defined the agenda and have been (unconsciously?) incorporated into charismatic theology of mission. Indeed, Bosch suggests that 'practically all contemporary schools of eschatology and of missionary thinking, in one way or another, are offshoots of the salvation-history approach'.[13]

I want to suggest that we develop existing charismatic understandings of eschatology to embrace some of these ideas. Yet we must not proceed before we consider some of the critiques that have been made of the 'salvation-historical' school. Perhaps the most forthright critique is that of Jürgen Moltmann, who sees this school as representing a 'kind of reduction of eschatology to historical time'.[14] Cullmann was trying to deal with the problem of the delayed parousia and overcame this by interpreting eschatology in this-worldly terms at the expense of the future dimension. In contrast Moltmann argues for an eschatology of the 'coming God' in attempting to keep both present and future dimensions in view at once. He does not like the simple 'linear time' assumed by Cullmann and others but rather argues that every moment in time has an eschatological sense: 'Every time is immediate to judgment, immediate to completion. In this sense, every time is last time. All time, not just the last time, will be perpetually ended and gathered up by eternity.'[15] The problem with Moltmann's approach is that he does not seem to appreciate fully the movement of time within which the present moment needs to be seen.[16] As Jeremy Begbie notes, 'there still *is* a fundamental "delay problem" in both Old and New Testaments which will not be solved simply by abandoning linear concepts of time and insisting that the parousia transforms time'.[17] So problems remain. Begbie suggests a way forward that I

---

[12] Thomas (ed.), *Readings*, 305.

[13] Bosch, *Transforming Mission*, 503–4.

[14] Richard Bauckham, 'Time and Eternity' in Richard Bauckham (ed.), *God Will be All in All: The Eschatology of Jürgen Moltmann* (Edinburgh: T&T Clark, 1999), 174; Jürgen Moltmann, *The Coming of God: Christian Eschatology* (London: SCM, 1996).

[15] Moltmann, *Coming*, 17.

[16] Bauckham, 'Time', 176.

[17] Jeremy S. Begbie, *Theology, Music and Time* (Cambridge: Cambridge University Press, 2000), 122.

think is worth utilising for our purposes here. Recognising the problems with 'crude linear models' of time yet recognising that time does have a linear element, Begbie suggests a model based on his study of music. Music is marked 'by multi-levelled patterns of equilibrium, tension and resolution'.[18] Of particular note for eschatology is the transition from tension to resolution that happens at different levels: within individual bars, through musical sections and throughout whole pieces of music. These can be represented graphically as below:[19]

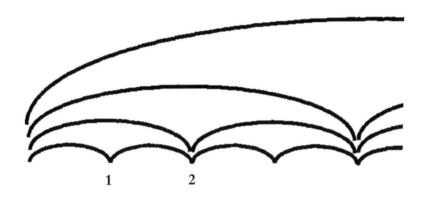

At point 1 a short phrase moves from tension to resolution (and then to tension again) and at point 2 both the short phrase and a larger phrase move from tension to resolution. The two even larger phrases are still in tension. Thus time is not seen to move simply from tension to resolution, but contains many levels of tension and of resolution. Using the metaphors I am developing in this book, time contains many levels of 'yearning' and 'blessing'. In terms of eschatology it is important to develop a framework that goes beyond some of the simplistic understanding of time often assumed in 'salvation-historical' approaches whilst appreciating the strengths of such approaches.

---

[18]   Ibid., 98.
[19]   Ibid., 106. Figure 4.1.

The Content of Mission

Where Begbie's approach is limited for our purposes is in its consideration of the 'end-time', although he does talk of 'final resolutions
prefigured'.[20] In considering the content of mission it is important to
ask about the nature of such 'final resolutions' or 'final blessings'
which we see coming into being in the present.[21] This approach is
different from a common pentecostal approach that starts from past
prophecy to look forward to determine future events.[22] The difficulty with such an approach is that it can end up embroiled in
speculative discussions over the interpretation of different prophecies and can be guilty of ignoring the holistic mission issues of the
present. Thus, for example, the tendency to back 'the restoration of
Israel, no matter what the means employed' ignores the vital issue of
justice for Palestinians.[23] If, instead, we focus on the words and
prophecies that speak of the coming 'new heavens and new earth'
(Rev. 21:1) we can gain a picture of a just, worshipping community
that can help direct change rather than simply speculation in the
present.

   As we have seen, some charismatic theology of mission does take
a broad approach to mission. But there is a need for a more thorough framework within which to understand the 'kingdom of God'
and the work of the mission of the Spirit and our part in it. Building
on Begbie's approach I want now to draw on the work of the biblical scholar Tom Wright, who has done much to outline early
Christian eschatology. Wright wants to move away from a simple
eschatology which talks of Christian hope in terms of 'going to

---

[20]   Ibid., 111.

[21]   This section develops some of my earlier thinking in 'Mission Eschatology: A Framework for Mission in the Spirit', *Journal of Pentecostal Theology* 11 (1997), 111–23.

[22]   Wilson suggests that this is the dominant Pentecostal understanding of
eschatology, although in terms of mission I think the understanding is
slightly broader, as outlined in Chapter 2. D.J. Wilson, 'Eschatology,
Pentecostal Perspectives on' in Burgess and van der Maas (eds.), *Dictionary
of Pentecostal and Charismatic Movements*, 601–5.

[23]   For more details of this debate from a mission perspective see my 'Mission, the Bible and Israel-Palestine', *Evangelical Review of Theology* 24.2
(2000), 149–58.

heaven when we die' towards a hope for 'new heavens and new earth, integrated together'.[24] The former understanding appears to look forward to an 'other-worldly' place with only loose connections with the present earth, time and space. This fits well with some approaches to evangelism but does seem rather gnostic in its desire to escape creation. Rather than this, Wright argues that we need to see 'heaven' as 'a *dimension*, normally kept secret, of present reality'.[25] God is 'constantly present' and 'gives his own breath to his human creation'.[26] Our final Christian hope is one of resurrection, seen not in disembodied personal terms, but rather as a renewed heavens and earth within which all pledge their allegiance to the one true God. This is the argument of Romans 8:18–28, which points to the renewal of the whole of creation, a renewal whose first fruits are tasted in the present by means of the Holy Spirit.

There are a number of dangers in this approach, notably that we might lose a sense of the movement of time and the radical nature of the coming new creation. So far it might appear that Wright falls into some of the traps of Moltmann in downplaying time. Whilst he does perhaps need to develop the theme of time in this regard, Wright does stress the radical nature of what is to come, talking of resurrection as 'a massive act of new creation'.[27] Christian hope is something looked forward to that is tasted in the present but only in a far-from-complete form. Elsewhere Wright speaks of heaven as 'the place where the divinely intended future for the world is kept safely in store'.[28] There is 'a two-sidedness to God-given, God-created reality' which might be called the 'earthly' and the 'heavenly'.[29] These will be integrated in the future by means of a radical resurrection that will affect the whole of creation. At the heart of this integration will be the personal presence of Jesus himself, 'the ultimate feature of Christian hope'.[30] Until then we wait,

---

[24] N.T. Wright, *New Heavens, New Earth: The Biblical Picture of Christian Hope* (Cambridge: Grove, 1999), 5.

[25] Ibid., 14.

[26] Ibid., 16.

[27] Ibid., 21.

[28] N.T. Wright, *The Resurrection of the Son of God* (London: SPCK, 2003), 368.

[29] N.T. Wright, *New Heavens*, 15.

[30] Ibid., 24.

glimpsing in the mission of the Spirit, in our mission, this integration of earthly and heavenly which is a powerfully attractive witness to Christ.

Let us now turn to some of the passages that speak of this future integration in a resurrected creation, the future 'kingdom of God' with Christ at the centre. In Revelation 7:9–17 we have a 'type scene' of a throne vision set in heaven that has much in common with Revelation 21:1 – 22:5.[31] Whilst there are a number of important interpretive issues in these passages, for our purposes I want to suggest that these passages give impressions of what the 'heavenly' is like. Issues such as the identification of the multitude and the period of time being seen are not crucial to our concerns here. Revelation 7:9–17 suggests that the heavenly includes worship; the end of hungering and thirsting (cf. Is. 49:10); Jesus at the centre (an application of the Davidic Messiah lamb motif to Jesus); and the end of sorrow and pain (wiping away tears, cf. Is. 25.8). Revelation 21 – 22 is notably different from Revelation 7 in the absence of the Temple, which is suggestive of a different time being viewed, but the overall picture is consistent. Again there is an end to sorrow and pain, with healing (21:4, 22:2); Jesus is at the centre, lighting all (21:23–24). There is also moral purity (21:27) and a new creation (21:1; cf. Is. 65:17, 66:22). We can link the centrality of Jesus here with the texts Ephesians 1:10 and Colossians 1:20, which speak of 'a restoration of harmony with Christ as the point of reintegration'.[32] There is much to debate in these verses, but we can see Christ is a focus for unity and reconciliation that encompasses the whole of creation.[33]

Much more space could be devoted to texts related to the 'heavenly' but this brief review is sufficient to give a broad picture encompassing:

(1)   the centrality of Jesus.
(2)   healing, without suffering or death.
(3)   perfect justice and peace.
(4)   unity in a diversity of people.
(5)   creation set free.

---

[31]   David E. Aune, *Revelation 6–16* (Dallas: Word, 1998).

[32]   Andrew T. Lincoln, *Ephesians* (Dallas: Word, 1998).

[33]   See also N.T. Wright, *Colossians and Philemon* (Leicester: Inter-Varsity Press, 1986), 78–9.

(6)   praise and worship.

(7)   love and fellowship.

This outline gains support from the wider studies of Stephen Travis and Moltmann who between them suggest the themes of peace, justice, equality, universality, respect for creation, love and fellowship.[34] If mission involves a movement of the Spirit to bring heavenly blessings into the present then this outline pictures a holistic vision for mission that encompasses:

(a)   evangelistic mission.

(b)   healing mission.

(c)   social mission.

(d)   reconciling mission.

(e)   ecological mission.

(f)   Christian spirituality.

(g)   Christian character and relationships.

It is interesting that Land's pentecostal understanding of the kingdom as characterised by gratitude (thanks, praise), compassion (love, longing) and courage (confidence, hope) relates to items (1), (6) and (7) in my outline – various essential elements of holistic mission are missing, which makes me question how useful his approach will be to a charismatic theology of mission. However, Land helpfully highlights the importance of congregational life to mission and items (6) and (7) are often absent from discussions on mission that focus on 'reaching out' separate from 'growing within'.

The suggested approach maintains the charismatic emphasis on eschatology whilst giving more detail and interacting more with the wider literature. It has the advantage over Grant McClung's alternative proposal in that it embraces a more holistic understanding of mission and is more integrated theologically. McClung maintains a simple understanding of eschatology related to an expectation of Christ's return and places word and Spirit at the centre.[35] The approach here also fits better with Jesus' understanding of his mission

---

[34] S.H. Travis, *I Believe in the Second Coming of Jesus* (London: Hodder & Stoughton, 1982); Jürgen Moltmann, 'A Pentecostal Theology of Life', *Journal of Pentecostal Theology* 9 (1996), 10–11. For more details see my 'Mission Eschatology', 113–14. Romans 8 is also in the background here.

[35] McClung Jr, 'Try', 45–7.

in the programmatic text of Luke 4:16–21, his words in the syna-
gogue at Nazareth. In this passage 'Luke' seems to be recounting the
same incident as in Mark 6:1–6, only he places it at the start of Jesus'
public ministry and gives much more detail. The new detail is
largely the quotation from Isaiah 61 with a verse from Isaiah 58 in
the middle. Within Luke's Gospel the use of Isaiah 61 is also seen in
Jesus' reply to John the Baptist (7:22–23) and we see Luke placing
Jesus' mission against a Jewish background of prophetic expectation. Much debate here centres on Christology: was Jesus an
anointed 'prophet' in the line of Moses (cf. 7:16 interpreted this
way), or an anointed messianic king in the line of David, or both, as
Max Turner argues?[36] However, for our purposes it is important to
note the eschatological background to this understanding of Jesus'
mission. The Qumran community understood Isaiah 61 in an eschatological way in 4Q521, although there it is God rather than
Jesus who carries out the mission. Max Turner suggests that the
Jewish hope for a 'New Exodus' forms the essential background for
Luke's understanding of Christ and salvation. This term has been
used in a number of ways but Turner uses it as 'a description of a
post-Exilic constellation of hopes developed from Isaiah 40–55'
that centres around 'Israel's deliverance from exile'.[37] This deliverance, or 'liberation from oppression' as Tom Wright sometimes
calls it,[38] was to come about through Jesus, who would bring the
new eschatological age to being in history. This was a 'this-worldly'
hope rather than a future eschatological hope.[39]

   The quotations from Isaiah do, on the face of it, provide a very
'social' and holistic understanding of Jesus' mission and the blessings
it would bring. Michael Prior argues that in particular the use of Isaiah 58 'intensifies the social dimension of the prophetic message,
and provides a striking corrective to any religious practice which
is carried on without concern for the poor'.[40] Clearly, the Old

---

[36] Max Turner, *Power from on High: The Spirit in Israel's Restoration and
Witness in Luke-Acts* (Sheffield: Sheffield Academic Press, 1996), 265–6.
[37] Ibid., 246.
[38] N.T. Wright, *The New Testament and the People of God* (London: SPCK,
1992), 299.
[39] Turner, *Power from on High*, 134.
[40] Michael Prior, *Jesus the Liberator: Nazareth Liberation Theology* (Sheffield: Sheffield Academic Press, 1995), 135.

Testament context suggests such a social understanding, and the key question here is what determines our exegesis.[41] Writers such as Turner stress, in contrast, the inter-testamental Jewish background and Luke's later detail of Jesus' ministry in 4:31–44. Here we seem to have a more metaphorical interpretation of Isaiah that focuses on exorcisms, healings and proclamation (especially 4:40–43). To 'proclaim release to the captives' (4:18) seems to relate more to release from demons, and 'recovery of sight to the blind' to physical healing. The focus on overcoming 'spiritual' evil continues through the Gospel, particularly in 8:26–39, 9:37–50 and 11:14–26. The latter is of particular importance as it regards a debate over the authority by which Jesus drove out demons. Rather than authority from Beelzebub, Jesus is seen to argue that his authority comes from God and that the exorcisms are linked with the coming of the 'kingdom of God'. Wright argues that in this passage (and others) the New Exodus hope is being redefined, so that rather than release from Roman occupation it is release from 'evil' in a more pervasive form, headed by 'the satan'.[42]

However, we are still left with the Old Testament background for Isaiah and the question as to whether it is completely metaphorical for Luke. Prior argues not, and in support of this we must note the importance of the themes of 'poor' and 'rich' for Luke. Unique to Luke is the banquet of the poor and disabled (14:12–14) and the parable of Lazarus (16:19–26). Luke also notes Jesus' concern for the Samaritans, Gentiles, women and tax collectors, who were less well regarded in the society of his time. Also, *plousios* (rich) occurs eleven times in Luke in contrast to twice in Mark and three times in Matthew. There are some stark contrasts made between rich and poor (e.g. 6:20, 24, 16:19, 21:1–4). Prior cites much evidence in support of this theme as being significant for Luke.[43] The 'New Exodus' motif, as used by Luke, seems to suggest a social and holistic understanding of mission, if one that is deepened by more reflection

---

[41] See also Brevard S. Childs, *Isaiah* (Louisville: Westminster John Knox Press, 2001), 506 who expounds this passage in the context after exile where the focus is more on 'release from economic slavery within the land'.

[42] N.T. Wright, *Jesus and the Victory of God*, (London: SPCK, 1996), 446–63.

[43] Prior, *Jesus the Liberator*, 163–83.

on the nature of evil. This debate supports my argument that Jesus' mission was holistic in nature, embracing the social as well as the spiritual.[44] It is a mission in line with bringing the 'kingdom of heaven' (as we have understood it) into being on earth.

The centrality of Jesus to any understanding of the 'heavenly' and the obvious overlap between the heavenly vision and the vision of Jesus' mission we see in Luke does imply that Christian mission must have the reality of Jesus at its heart. This may seem obvious, but it does imply that evangelism has a certain kind of priority in mission, something that is controversial in some circles. Evangelicals have had heated debates on this subject and a number of ways of bringing together evangelism and social action as part of a holistic understanding of mission have been attempted. Rather than enter fully into the debate at this point it is worth noting that my way through the impasse is similar to that suggested by Ronald Sider, who expounds the eschatological kingdom.[45] However, I extend Sider's outlook to embrace more fully details of the future kingdom and to go beyond 'evangelism' and 'social action' to consider wider aspects of mission. Tim Dakin's phrase 'holistic evangelism' is worth exploring further in this regard – evangelism seen not just through proclamation, but through healing, moves to justice, searching after unity, caring for creation, and in the life of congregations.[46] In this sense, 'holistic evangelism' is about the 'holistic centrality of Christ' to all mission in this world.

The Spirit and Mission

We now turn to an understanding of the Holy Spirit as the means by which the universal eschatological blessings are brought to life in

---

[44] It is also interesting to reflect on the extent to which scholars' understandings of mission might be influencing their reading of the text at this point – those more likely to focus on evangelism seem to ignore the social in Luke; those focusing on the social tend to ignore the healings and exorcisms and the evangelism.

[45] Ronald Sider, *Evangelism and Social Action* (London: Hodder & Stoughton, 1993).

[46] Term used within the Church Mission Society (CMS). Tim Dakin is General Secretary of CMS, UK.

particular individuals and communities in the world. Having considered Luke's Gospel, it is worth first considering the Spirit as the 'anointer' and 'director' of Jesus' mission. The key text of Luke 4:18 is taken word-for-word from the LXX: 'The Spirit of the Lord is upon me.' The New Exodus is a time of the Spirit, a theme also seen in Luke's presentation of Jesus' temptations which Max Turner links with the time Israel spent in the wilderness.[47] Luke emphasises the Spirit through an *inclusio* (4:1, 14) and the apparent suggestion that the Spirit was with Jesus in the wilderness and not just in the initial directing (Luke's use of *en* compared to *eis* in Mark). Obviously a number of themes are being woven together within which the Spirit and Exodus is important. Recent scholarship has been somewhat torn between understanding Luke's portrayal of the Spirit in terms of 'sonship' or 'empowering'.[48] In response to the history of religions approach, F. Büchsel stressed the 'Spirit of Sonship' as a bridge between Jesus and the early church. H. von Baer emphasised the 'empowering Spirit' as this bridge based on a three-epoch understanding of salvation history. More recently James Dunn has seen the Spirit as the source of sonship and covenant life, although many scholars, such as E. Schweizer, R.P. Menzies and R. Stronstrad, have now moved to stress the 'empowering Spirit' especially through the matrix of understanding termed 'the Spirit of Prophecy': an understanding seen to be common in inter-testamental Judaism. However, definitions of this 'Spirit of Prophecy' have been seen to be too narrow, focusing on 'prophetic speech and revelation'.[49] Luke's understanding appears broader and so attempts are being made to reflect this breadth by J.B. Shelton, H.S. Kim, G. Haya-Prats and Turner. Having already suggested the need for a liberationist as well as a metaphorical understanding of Luke 4:16–21, I am clearly going along with this broader approach. In particular, Turner argues that the sources also allow for the 'Spirit of prophecy' to encompass power, ethics and salvation.[50] Under this latter category of 'salvation' it is important for our purposes to understand the work of the Spirit in

---

[47] Turner, *Power from on High*, 134.
[48] See the detailed overview in ibid., 20–81.
[49] As most clearly seen in Luke 1:41ff., 1:67ff., 1:15, 1:35 etc.
[50] Turner, *Power from on High*, 82–138.

bringing in the holistic salvation of the New Exodus, or, in my language, bringing the blessings of the heavenly kingdom through mission.[51]

This working of the Spirit in the mission of Jesus can also be seen in the mission of the disciples. In Luke–Acts a number of scholars have noted the similarities between the presentation of Jesus in the Gospel and those of Stephen, Peter and Paul in Acts. Martin Dibelius no doubt overstates the case in suggesting that the author presents Jesus as a Jewish martyr as was common in some of the literature of the time.[52] Yet Jesus as a model for discipleship does seem an important key in understanding Luke–Acts, with a recognition that discipleship will involve persecution and perhaps death. Jesus is seen as a model for the discipleship of particular Christian leaders, yet his teaching is also seen as the basis for the discipleship of the new communities that come into prominence in Acts.[53] Bock summarises Luke's aim as teaching that 'being a disciple is not easy, but it is full of rich blessing which transcends anything else this life can offer'.[54] It is important to bring the themes of suffering and blessings together as Bock does. For as Matthew has it: 'Blessed are those who are persecuted because of righteousness, for theirs is the kingdom of heaven' (5:10). The blessings of God even encompass persecution, suffering and yearning. We cannot pretend that the Spirit will lead us into a life of blessings separate from a life also of suffering. The 'Spirit of Christ' cannot but lead us into the fullness of Jesus' experience that is filled with both blessings and yearnings: the Spirit and the cross belong together.

---

[51]   See the brief reflections of Turner that link with the work of Wright: *Power from on High*, 133–6. See also Stanton's summary of Luke's presentation as 'God's way triumphs', *The Gospels and Jesus* (Oxford: Oxford University Press, 2002), 79ff.

[52]   Brian E. Beck, '*Imitatio Christi* and the Lucan Passion Narrative' in William Horbury and Brian McNeil (eds.), *Suffering and Martyrdom in the New Testament* (Cambridge: Cambridge University Press, 1981), 28–47.

[53]   D.L. Bock, 'Luke, Gospel of' in Joel B. Green, Scot McKnight and I. Howard Marshall (eds.), *Dictionary of Jesus and the Gospels* (Leicester: Inter-Varsity Press, 1992), 506–7.

[54]   Ibid., 509.

Mission and Opposition

So far I have suggested that it is by the Holy Spirit that disciples bring the blessings of the 'heavenly' kingdom to birth in the world today. This is a mission that reflects that of Jesus and hence is also characterised by a suffering that includes a yearning over situations where blessings are not in evidence. In Matthew's Gospel this yearning is seen in the tension between Jesus and some of the Jewish leaders, often linked with the Christological title 'son of David'. After the healing of the blind men who call on the 'son of David' the Pharisees accuse Jesus: 'It is by the prince of demons that he drives out demons' (9:34). This theme is again picked up after another healing of a man born blind and mute which provokes questions about the 'son of David' (12:23). Again the Pharisees say that Jesus is healing through the prince of demons, to which Jesus responds with a detailed rebuff (12:24–37). The final healing linked with the 'son of David' comes just before the triumphal entry after which the 'chief priests and the teachers of the law' were indignant that the children were acclaiming Jesus as 'son of David' (21:14–16). Graham Stanton concludes from these passages that there was 'fierce opposition' to claims that Jesus was the Davidic Messiah.[55] This supports his argument for a strong divide between the Christian communities Matthew is writing to and the Jewish leaders. As D. Verseput states, 'we can affirm with little hesitation that the decisive christological category inciting the Jewish opposition in Matthew's Gospel is that of the Davidic Messiah'.[56] However, although I agree that the conflict motif is significant I would not want to read as much into these passages as Stanton does. We need to note how this term is used in regard to incidents of healing, particularly of healing the blind (Mt. 9:27, 12:23, 15:22, 20:30, 31). That the 'son of David' came to heal probably has roots in the Old Testament, as Peter Head argues, but its emphasis for Matthew represents a reworked understanding of the title.[57] Also, Matthew does not present Jesus as

---

[55] Graham N. Stanton, *A Gospel for a New People: Studies in Matthew* (Edinburgh: T&T Clark, 1992), 185.

[56] D. Verseput, 'The Role and Meaning of the "Son of God" Title in Matthew's Gospel', *New Testament Studies* 33.4 (1987), 536.

[57] Peter M. Head, *Christology and the Synoptic Problem: An Argument for Markan Priority* (Cambridge: Cambridge University Press, 1997), 182–4; John Riches, *Matthew* (Sheffield: Sheffield Academic Press, 1996), 100.

fulfilling the political expectations of the people, but rather as the
humble king acclaimed as 'son of David' as he rode into Jerusalem
on a donkey (21:9). True, following on from this Jesus cleansed the
Temple, which was a royal action (21:15).[58] This links with Jesus as
'Lord', 'a divine predicate of majesty'.[59] But the action quickly
moves on to the parable of the Tenants, which indicates Jesus' suffering and death (21:33–46) and the woes against the 'teachers of the
law and Pharisees' (23:23). Jesus' mission aroused opposition regarding his kingship as 'son of David' but his approach was one of
humility and suffering – in my language, one of yearning that
brought blessings not by imposition or aggression but through faith.

C. Peter Wagner, in his charismatic understanding of 'spiritual
warfare', points to Matthew 11:12, 'the kingdom of heaven suffers
violence, and violent men take it by force' (NASB). This he inter-
prets with regard to a battle between Satan and Jesus:

> Satan is referred to several times as the god of this age or the prince of
> the power of the air. He has usurped God's authority and set up his
> kingdom here on earth. His power is awesome … When Jesus came
> He invaded Satan's kingdom with the kingdom of God … He is not
> taking this invasion lying down. That is why violence has erupted both
> in the heavenlies and here on earth.[60]

Donald Hagner suggests that this verse is about the suffering and
persecution that comes with the kingdom, as in evidence for the
Christians of Matthew's day. He suggests, following Davies and
Allison, that forces of evil may lie behind this opposition but does
not focus on these as Wagner does.[61] In support of a more spiritual
interpretation Wagner turns to Colossians 2:15: 'He disarmed the
rulers and authorities and made a public example of them, triumph-
ing over them in it.' The theological basis, for Wagner, of the
Christian victory over the powers of evil is found in the cross of
Christ as particularly seen in Colossians. For him the devil and de-

---

[58] N.T. Wright, *Jesus*, 490–93.

[59] Head, *Christology*, 165.

[60] C. Peter Wagner (ed.), *Territorial Spirits* (Chichester: Sovereign World,
1991), 5.

[61] Donald A. Hagner, *Matthew 1–13* (Dallas: Word, 1998), commentary
on verse.

mons are in a spiritual battle against Christians and we need to fight back using 'spiritual weapons'.[62]

Although it is common in charismatic circles to take such a spiritual interpretation of the opposition to mission, it is not clear that the verses used can carry the weight of such an interpretation. More conservative evangelicals have tended to interpret the Colossians verse in terms of Christ's victory over the evil of individual sin and his ability to forgive and make people alive in Christ.[63] Yet such an individualised interpretation does not seem to fit with the cosmic vision of Christ presented in 1:15–20. For a more holistic way forward that fits with the earlier consideration of the nature of mission it is useful to turn again to Wright. His desire is to hold together the 'heavenly' and the 'earthly' as we have seen. In the Gospels, he suggests, we see Jesus re-telling a crucial Jewish story in a new way:

> Israel's story had sometimes been told in terms of four great empires that had oppressed her. The last one would eventually be destroyed when her god finally acted to bring in his kingdom. In first-century Jewish retellings of this story the fourth kingdom was bound to be Rome. But Rome, from Jesus' point of view, could be at most the penultimate enemy. The pagan hordes surrounding Israel were not the actual foe of the people of YHWH. Standing behind the whole problem of Israel's exile was the dark power known in some Old Testament traditions as the satan, the accuser. The struggle that was coming to a head was therefore cosmic, not merely martial …[64]

Here we find a way forward in obtaining a more holistic charismatic understanding of opposition to mission – an opposition that is spiritual but not in a way that is separate from the material. Within this outlook of course there will be opposition to people individually being freed from sin but the picture is much bigger and it was the big picture that was in the minds of people in Jesus' day. Wright also usefully extends Wagner's focus on the cross to include the evidence of Jesus' ministry. He suggests that Jesus' victory began in the

---

[62] Wagner (ed.), *Territorial Spirits*, 7.

[63] E.g. see Peter T. O'Brien, *Colossians, Philemon* (Dallas: Word, 1998), commentary on Colossians 2:15.

[64] N.T. Wright, *Jesus*, 451.

desert as he overcame Satan's temptations and is seen in his ministry
of overcoming evil. All these point to the climax of a 'final battle' he
had to fight alone on the cross to overcome the dark powers.[65]
Wright's understanding of Colossians 2:15 focuses more on the
'earthly' than the 'heavenly': 'there is nothing in the passage which
warrants understanding the "powers" as (what we think of as) "the
powers of evil," identical with Satan and his angels'.[66] They are
more naturally thought of as representing the rulers and authorities
of Rome and of Israel, although these 'had come to embody the re-
bellion of the world'.[67]

Wright's outlook here is similar to that of Walter Wink, who is
concerned to hold together the heavenly and the earthly. In defining the 'Powers' based on the biblical witness he suggests that they
are the inner aspect of material reality: 'We encounter them primarily in reference to the material or "earthly" reality of which they are
the innermost essence.'[68] These Powers are good but fallen and so
must be redeemed. This redemption comes through Jesus, who
came 'to destroy the devil's work' (1 Jn. 3:8) in 'a cosmic battle in
which Jesus rescues humanity from the dominion of evil powers'.[69]
This outlook enables Wink to keep the priority of both prayer and
social action, the heavenly and the earthly, in a context that is realis-
tic as regards the opposition we face in mission. However, as Yong
points out, 'Wink seems ultimately to reduce the demonic to social,
institutional, or organizational realities' in a way that overlaps with
but does not embrace the whole of charismatic experience.[70] What
is needed is a model that allows for the 'multidimensionality of the
demonic' within which evil opposition to mission can take a variety
of forms as the heavenly and the earthly interact in a multitude of
ways. The temptation is to simplify things: to suggest that opposition is always aimed at preventing conversion to Christ, or is always

---

[65] Ibid., 457, 463, 466.

[66] N.T. Wright, *Colossians and Philemon*, 115.

[67] Ibid., 117.

[68] Walter Wink, *Naming the Powers: The Language of Power in the New Testament* (Philadelphia: Fortress Press, 1984), 105.

[69] Ibid., 26.

[70] Amos Yong, *Beyond the Impasse: Toward a Pneumatological Theology of
Religion* (Carlisle: Paternoster, 2003), 137.

of a 'spiritual' nature, or is always of a socio-political nature. In contrast I am arguing for a holistic approach to opposition that reflects a holistic approach to mission. In this the yearnings felt in opposition interact with the blessings seen in mission.

Summary of Themes

In this chapter I have broadened the traditional charismatic understanding of eschatology in order to gain a more holistic understanding of mission. The mission of the Spirit is to bring the holistic blessings of the eschatological kingdom into the world today. It is also about the yearnings seen in the absence of such blessings and the presence of opposition. It is the Holy Spirit who continues to stretch our horizons and open us up evermore to the greatness and the yearnings of God.

5

Experiential Mission

I had been taught to be highly suspicious of 'experience' and 'subjective Christianity'. God was often portrayed to be great, but remote ... Now something was happening to me; something that could only be described as 'experience'. I felt different. I *was* different. I was bubbling over with joy. It seemed as if the whole room, the whole house, everyone and everything around me had changed.[1]

Whenever we stand together in church and pray, 'Come, Holy Spirit,' we affirm that our God is the God who comes; we lift our faith and wait expectantly for him to come ... It is always much easier to believe in the God who came and will come again, than in the God who comes.[2]

There is some hesitation in seeing religious experience as a key source for theology and for good reasons.[3] Without here wanting to enter into this wider debate it is impossible to avoid the importance of religious experience to charismatic mission practice and theological reflection. For Colin Urquhart, as for many charismatics, a turning point in their lives is seen to be when what had been mainly something just thought about became something experienced. In the 'charismatic creed' of Jan Veenhof: 'God can be experienced in

---

[1] Colin Urquhart, *When the Spirit Comes* (London: Hodder & Stoughton, 1974), 9.
[2] Peter H. Lawrence, *Doing What Comes Supernaturally* (Bristol: Terra Nova, 1997), 54.
[3] See, for example, the introductory critique of Alister McGrath, *Christian Theology: An Introduction* (Oxford: Blackwell, 1997), 223–31.

Jesus through the Spirit today, by the entire person!"[4] Charismatic mission is not something thought about but something experienced in a holistic way today, something that changes lives for the better. For Peter Lawrence and others the experiential prayer 'Come, Holy Spirit' can be seen to sum up charismatic missiology. This fits with the movement of the Spirit from the universal eschatological kingdom to the particular seen in the last chapter. Yet this alone can underplay the value of everyday experience and God's working in all things, not just in the extraordinary. It is important that we consider the importance of experience as a possible starting point and not just the end point. This can be usefully done through an examination of a dialogue that took place between pentecostal scholars and Jürgen Moltmann. Such a dialogue took place in the *Journal of Pentecostal Theology* and highlights the differences on this issue. The dialogue also contributes more detailed understanding to the framework for the mission of the Spirit that I am developing.

The 'Particular' and the 'Universal' in Mission[5]

In the framework we see movements of the Spirit between the 'particular' and the 'universal'. Here we note both the particular eschatological working of the Holy Spirit and the universal creative work of the Spirit in the whole of life. The theological tension that can be found between these two is also seen in the different stress given either to the transcendent or to the immanent workings of God by different scholars. I want to survey the dialogue in the context of our present concern for mission and against some of the wider mission thinking. We are here asking how the blessings of mission outlined in the last chapter are experienced in the life of the church and the world, aware that different people stress different kinds of blessing.

---

[4] Jan Veenhof, 'The Significance of the Charismatic Renewal for Theology and Church' in Jan A. B. Jongeneel (ed.), *Pentecost, Mission and Ecumenism* (Frankfurt: Peter Lang, 1992), 297.

[5] An earlier version of the next sections appeared in Andrew M. Lord, 'The Moltmann-Pentecostal Dialogue: Implications for Mission', *Journal of Pentecostal Theology* 11.2 (2003), 271–87.

In the dialogue pentecostal scholars focus on the 'particular' and challenge what they see as the universalising tendency of Moltmann. This challenge is often focused against Moltmann's association of the Spirit with the whole of creation. Simon Chan appeals to C.F.D. Moule to support his claim that 'the idea of the *creator spiritus* is not really the main focus of the canonical writings'[6] but rather the focus of the Spirit is within the fellowship of God's people, the church. Chan allows for 'different degrees of the Spirit's personal presence' but feels that Moltmann gives in to 'a tendency to "diffuse" the personality of the Spirit in the world'.[7] He critiques Moltmann's construction of a 'streaming personhood' of the Spirit as lacking a distinct focus for the person of the Spirit. A distinct focus is what Chan sees as being required by the biblical witness and for a proper appreciation of the role of the Spirit within the church. In response Moltmann points firstly to his development of a pneumatological ecclesiology elsewhere, which the pentecostal scholars do not address.[8] However, Frank Macchia challenges this on the basis that Moltmann's pneumatology has developed over time and so it is not satisfactory just to point to earlier works, and surely Moltmann could have developed his earlier pneumatology more as it relates to the mission of the church.[9] As regards the personality of the Spirit, Moltmann points to his exposition of the Spirit as the personal Liberator, Comforter and Judge. Even so, Macchia suggests that there is an ambivalence in Moltmann's expressions of the Spirit as distinct from life (to avoid pantheism) yet often seemingly identified with life.[10] The debate here seems more one of emphasis: Chan and Macchia want to emphasise personhood distinct from creation whereas for Moltmann this is just the starting point for a universal understanding of the Spirit that emphasises creation. Moltmann appears to start with the 'particulars' of personhood and church and quickly moves in the direction of the

---

[6] C.F.D. Moule, *The Holy Spirit* (London: Mowbrays, 1978), 7–21.

[7] Simon Chan, 'An Asian Review [of *Spirit of Life*]', *Journal of Pentecostal Theology* 4 (1994), 39.

[8] Jürgen Moltmann, 'A Response to my Pentecostal Dialogue Partners', *Journal of Pentecostal Theology* 4 (1994), 60.

[9] Frank D. Macchia, 'The Spirit and Life: A Further Response to Jürgen Moltmann', *Journal of Pentecostal Theology* 5 (1994), 126–7.

[10] Ibid., 123–4.

'universal' whereas pentecostal scholars move quickly from the universal future kingdom back to the particular of the church. The gap in the pentecostal approach is identified by Juan Sepúlveda who states that there is a 'total absence in Pentecostalism of a theology of creation'.[11] This is a lack of movement from the particular to the universal and hence Moltmann argues that 'the theology of Pentecostal experience must lead to a theology of creation "in the Holy Spirit"'.[12]

Mark Stibbe quotes E. Schweizer's argument that the Bible does not support an understanding of the Spirit at work in the entire creation, and finds Moltmann's biblical exegesis severely limited.[13] This latter point is taken up in a later debate between Richard Bauckham and Moltmann in which Moltmann argues that it is valid for him to take a *theological* rather than a *literal* approach.[14] Interestingly, here Stibbe (and Macchia) argue for a 'universal' canonical approach to the Bible whereas Moltmann argues in favour of a particular stress on the Pauline corpus.[15] Stibbe does allow for the possibility of the Spirit at work in creation, and suggests that Moltmann could also have considered the Spirit at work in 'art, literature, philosophy, mathematics and science'.[16] However, he appears to misunderstand Moltmann to be saying that creation is full of 'the vitalizing energies of Spirit' with no 'demonic energies'. From this perspective he concludes that Moltmann's outlook sees all people as 'anonymous Christians' (Karl Rahner) and even as 'anonymous charismatics' in a way that makes mission and evangelism pointless. Stibbe points to the need for discernment. However, Moltmann does acknowledge the deep reality of death in the world and the need for conversion and liberation. Here Moltmann sees Stibbe's approach as suggesting a dualism between salvation and creation. Moltmann is at pains to overcome this ontological dualism

---

[11] Juan Sepúlveda, 'The Perspective of Chilean Pentecostalism [on *Spirit of Life*]', *Journal of Pentecostal Theology* 4 (1994), 48.

[12] Moltmann, 'Response', 62.

[13] Eduard Schweizer, 'On Distinguishing between Spirits', *Ecumenical Review* 41.3 (July 1989), 408; Stibbe, 'British', 15–16.

[14] Jürgen Moltmann, 'The Bible, the Exegete and the Theologian' in Bauckham (ed.), *God Will be All in All*, 229–30.

[15] Macchia, 'Further Response', 126; Moltmann, 'Response', 66–7.

[16] Stibbe, 'British', 14.

by stressing the *apocalyptic* dualism between 'this crooked world' and 'the new, just world, which is coming' which gives rise to the need for liberation.[17] For him the criterion for discernment is ultimately the cross of Christ: 'Whatever can endure when it is confronted with the Crucified is Spirit from his Spirit.'[18] Perhaps again there is a difference in emphasis, with Moltmann emphasising evil in the world as a whole is overcome through liberation and Stibbe emphasising personal evil that needs overcoming through conversion. From a South African perspective, Japie Lapoorta supports Moltmann's attempt to overcome dualisms that tend towards the gnostic. He links this attempt with African spirituality in which he sees 'the presence of the Holy Spirit … [that] permeates all spheres of life'.[19]

A more personal and passionate appeal comes from Peter Kuzmic, who argues against Moltmann's stress on the universal Spirit of life through an argument linked with his personal narrative of life in a war situation. Kuzmic's experience in Bosnia is of oppression, bloodshed, refugees – 'the death of humanity' which seemed to imply 'the death of the ecumenical political theology and its utopian dreams'.[20] This experience leads Kuzmic to critique Moltmann's 'implicit optimism in regard to human will and nature' and stress rather the particular need for redemption and repentance. Here the question is to what extent the building of a 'universal culture of life' is possible. Moltmann takes Kuzmic's argument as 'blind, indiscriminate aggression' and points to his chapter on justification in which he deals with the victims and perpetrators of violence with reference to God's atonement.[21] The dialogue here does not get beyond feelings of offence, despite a key issue being raised. Whereas Moltmann argues for a 'universal affirmation of life' (cf. subtitle of the *Spirit of Life*), Kuzmic argues that reality is more a 'universal affirmation of death'. Moltmann's universal affirmation

---

[17] Moltmann, 'Response', 63.

[18] Ibid., 67.

[19] Japie J. Lapoorta, 'An African Perspective [on *Spirit of Life*]', *Journal of Pentecostal Theology* 4 (1994), 52–3, 57.

[20] Peter Kuzmic, 'A Croatian-War-Time Reading [of *Spirit of Life*]', *Journal of Pentecostal Theology* 4 (1994), 19, 20.

[21] Moltmann, 'Response', 68–9.

requires the Spirit to be at work in creation, whereas Kuzmic's universal affirmation requires the Spirit to be at work in individual redemption from sin. Moltmann prefers to talk of 'the God of the godless' whose mercy envelopes the perpetrators of violence, whereas Kuzmic stresses the need for perpetrators to repent.[22] Again, neither view totally excludes the other but represents a significant difference in emphasis that springs from different contexts.

This contrast of emphasis is reflected in some of the wider debates in mission. For many years mission focused on personal conversion alongside the doctrinal view, summarised by Hendrikus Berkhof, that 'personal salvation has been considered the main goal of the Spirit'.[23] This focus developed over the last century to an emphasis on the church viewed as essentially missionary.[24] The development of interest from church to creation has come only recently, with Andrew Kirk commenting in 1999 how 'environmental matters are seldom linked to mission'.[25] A notable exception to this has been the mission reflection of the World Council of Churches (WCC) that asserted in 1983 that 'peace, justice and the integrity of creation belong together'. Moltmann worked with the WCC and his outlook picks up the themes of creation and the Spirit in a similar way, although he resists Stibbe's portrayal of him as just an elaborator of the WCC theology of mission.[26]

The tension between pentecostal scholars and Moltmann over the means of mission reflects, in part, some of the tensions between evangelicals and the (ecumenical) WCC. Ecumenical approaches to mission are often contrasted with evangelical approaches as represented by the Lausanne-related meetings. Many evangelicals trace the divergence between Lausanne and the WCC to the 1958 Ghana assembly at which the decision was made to integrate the Interna-

---

[22] Jürgen Moltmann, *The Spirit of Life* (London: SCM, 1992), 137; Kuzmic, 'Croatian-War-Time', 19.

[23] Hendrikus Berkhof, *The Doctrine of the Holy Spirit* (London: Epworth Press, 1965), 40.

[24] Bosch, *Transforming Mission*, 368–73.

[25] Andrew J. Kirk, *What is Mission? Theological Explorations* (London: Darton, Longman & Todd, 1999), 166.

[26] Moltmann, 'Response', 61; Stibbe, 'British', 16.

tional Missionary Council into the WCC. Timothy Yates outlines
how this divergence grew in the 1960s and 1970s.[27] Alan Bailyes
suggests that the two main differences between these approaches are
seen in their approach to ecclesiology and conversion. Ecumenical
understandings stress that God's concern is not primarily with the
church but with humanity as a whole. Consequently, 'mission' must
aim at the 'humanisation of society'.[28] Rather than individual conversion ecumenical understandings stressed liberation and dialogue.
In contrast, evangelical understandings put conversion central, with
the church 'regarded first and foremost as a community of the
redeemed' in contrast to the 'unholy world'. Both Yates and Bailyes
comment on the common desire for mission that is holistic in
nature, but point to continuing tensions. This study of the
Moltmann–pentecostal dialogue contributes to an understanding of
these tensions in terms of the pneumatological differences between
the two outlooks.

This dialogue only touches on some of the thinking of
Moltmann and pentecostal scholars. I noted earlier how pentecostal
eschatology has tended to focus on the inauguration of the eschatological kingdom and the imminent return of Jesus. This idea was
developed in the last chapter to show how a holistic understanding
of the eschatological kingdom can lead to a holistic view of Christian mission in the present. The mission of the Spirit was seen as
moving *from* the universal eschatological kingdom to particular individuals and communities. In the dialogue we are now
considering, Moltmann effectively challenges pentecostals to appreciate the counter-movement *towards* the eschatological
kingdom. Moltmann's wider theology maintains 'a strongly
christological center in the particular history of Jesus and at the same
time a universal direction'.[29] Richard Bauckham suggests that it is
Moltmann's emphasis on the future eschatological orientation of
theology that is his most significant contribution.[30] Hence, it is not

---

[27] Timothy Yates, *Christian Mission in the Twentieth Century* (Cambridge:
Cambridge University Press, 1994), 193–200.
[28] Alan J. Bailyes, 'Evangelical and Ecumenical Understandings of Mission', *International Review of Mission* 85.339 (1996), 488.
[29] Richard Bauckham, 'Jürgen Moltmann' in David F. Ford (ed.), *The
Modern Theologians* (Oxford: Blackwell, 1997), 211.
[30] Ibid., 213.

surprising that Moltmann characterises mission primarily under the heading 'mission looking towards the end'.[31] He considers the 'mission of the Spirit' as a 'movement of life' that is concerned with God's kingdom and the world. The movement towards the eschatological kingdom is a movement that embraces the world. Moltmann challenges us to develop an 'integrative eschatology' within which the universal creation is seen as moving towards God's future.[32] Eschatological hope is progressive, starting with the resurrection of Jesus and moving forward in ever-expanding circles that embrace individuals, communities, nations and the whole of creation.[33] The tension and challenge here is between a focus on the universal experience and work of the Spirit in all of life as opposed to one focused on the particular work of the Spirit in individuals and the church. It is the tension between these two emphases that characterises the dialogue and helps give a pneumatological understanding of the tensions in wider mission thinking. In terms of the framework I am developing, I want to suggest that we need to appreciate both the movements of the Spirit toward the universal and those toward the particular.

The 'Transcendent' and the 'Immanent' in Mission

The tension between the 'particular' and the 'universal' can also be seen as a tension between stressing God's transcendence or immanence. The pentecostal scholars critique Moltmann not only for his stress on the universal but also on the immanent nature of God. Simon Chan argues that Moltmann's view of the experience of God as 'immanent transcendence' represents the philosophical foundation for his pneumatology. This is a 'panentheistic conception of God' in which 'there is no separation between the "supernatural" and the "natural" charismata'.[34] Chan sees this stress on immanence as very positively overcoming false dualisms and yet he argues that

---

[31] Jürgen Moltmann, 'The Mission of the Spirit: The Gospel of Life' in Yates (ed.), *Mission*, 24.
[32] Richard Bauckham, 'Eschatology in *The Coming of God*' in Bauckham (ed.), *God Will be All in All*, 10.
[33] Ibid., 20–21.
[34] Chan, 'Asian', 38.

'Moltmann has not sufficiently stressed the transcendent dimension … Not that the transcendent dimension is missing, but it is experienced through immanence.'[35] Rather than a stress on universal immanence Chan wants to stress the particular transcendent, holy, Spirit within the church. For him, Moltmann's emphasis on universal immanence does not allow the Holy Spirit to be differentiated from the 'other spirits' common in the Asian context. Kuzmic also appreciates Moltmann's attempt to overcome false dualisms, but feels that 'the resultant blending of the supernatural and the natural may not result in a corrective balancing but in an unholy blurring'.[36] He sees Moltmann as overreacting against Barth in attempting 'a synthesis between what is immanent and what is transcendent' that results in 'a pneumatology that is more humanistic than Christian and more political than theological'.[37] Kuzmic does not put forward an adequate alternative proposal, but rather stresses 'the biblical centrality of the Spirit's work in redemption', which suggests that for him the transcendent nature of the Spirit is key in order for redemption to remain central.

Macchia starts by stating that the 'experience of the Spirit as immanent in life is at the very heart of the book [*Spirit of Life*]' for Moltmann. Hence, Moltmann 'passionately resists theological transcendentalism which views God as Wholly Other [Barth]'.[38] It is this resistance to God's 'otherness' that is the basic problem that Macchia sees pentecostals as having with Moltmann's pneumatology.[39] This transcendent 'otherness' Macchia defines in terms of Barth's 'Wholly Other' and Otto's 'fascinating and terrifying mystery'. He identifies the key pentecostal experience as that of the 'terrifying mystery' and is not convinced that Moltmann embraces such experiences in his definition of 'immanent transcendence'. These experiences are of 'confrontation' that challenge evil in people and in the world. Such evil, argues Macchia, requires a greater distinction between transcendence and immanence than Moltmann allows. Although Macchia finds 'Moltmann's vision of

---

[35] Ibid.

[36] Kuzmic, 'Croatian-War-Time', 22.

[37] Ibid., 23.

[38] Frank D. Macchia, 'A North American Response [to *Spirit of Life*]', *Journal of Pentecostal Theology* 4 (1994), 25.

[39] Ibid., 26.

the Spirit as the womb of life' appealing, he feels that in order for the Spirit to be involved in creating and sustaining life it is not necessary to follow 'Moltmann in identifying the Spirit with the essence of created life'.[40] After all, even Moltmann 'advocates an ecstatic experience of God through the Spirit that "interrupts" the divine-human interaction implied in the liturgy'.[41]

Macchia's argument is that if God through the Spirit is free to interrupt and confront creation then he cannot be completely identified with that creation in the way 'immanent transcendence' implies. This argument links well with the important questions posed by Stibbe: 'In what sense is the Spirit of God immanent or present within the created order? … If the Spirit of God is active in creation, is he already present, or only when people invoke his presence?'[42] Stibbe and Macchia argue that the Spirit of God is active in creation through particular transcendent experiences, notably those characteristic within the pentecostal movement. This is consistent with the pentecostal theology of mission with its 'radical strategy' based on particular 'divine interventions in signs and wonders'.[43] Pentecostal scholars are keen not to lose this transcendent focus even though they allow for the Spirit to be at work more generally in creation. How to define this is far from easy and I will return to this in considering Amos Yong in the next chapter.

In response Moltmann asserts that pentecostal experience of the Holy Spirit 'has to do with the soul and the body, with salvation and healing' despite the different interpretations of that experience given by the pentecostal scholars seen above that emphasise Barth's 'Wholly Other'.[44] Moltmann outlines Barth's understanding but bluntly states: 'That is not my experience of God.'[45] Here the key difference is one of experience rather than theology. Moltmann goes on to argue that pentecostal theology 'must begin with the Spirit's immanence', his 'indwelling' in creation and 'must lead to a theology of creation'.[46] For Moltmann, the emphasis on imma-

---

[40] Ibid., 29.
[41] Ibid., 30.
[42] Stibbe, 'British', 12.
[43] McGee, 'Power'.
[44] Moltmann, 'Response', 62.
[45] Ibid., 65.
[46] Ibid., 64.

nence came in reaction against 'Barth's transcendental theology of
the "Wholly Other"' although he wants to keep 'Barth's presence'
in order to avoid the one-sidedness that pentecostal scholars accuse
him of.[47] How Barth's understanding of the transcendent can be
linked with Moltmann's emphasis on the immanent is left unex-
plored, and they seem disjointed in the *Spirit of Life*.[48] Moltmann
admits to not having emphasised the transcendent because he does
not consider this a 'theological category' that pertains to God:
'Heaven is transcendent as opposed to earth, but not God, the Creator of heaven and earth.'[49] As regards God, the sense of God being
'far-away' that pentecostals seem to stress is for Moltmann found in
the Old Testament and thus not relevant for today since the 'Father
of Jesus Christ … is so close to us'.[50]

Clearly, the definition of 'transcendence' is important here and
Macchia clarifies his position in his further response to Moltmann.
Macchia sees himself as attempting to reinterpret Barth's understanding of the 'Wholly Other' in the context of his 'experience of
the *eschatological Spirit* in worship'.[51] Thus Macchia is not wanting to
identify pentecostals with Barth and can see Moltmann's stress on
the immanent Spirit as significant for the development of pentecostal pneumatology. However, he does not feel that Moltmann
stresses sufficiently 'the eschatological freedom and criticism exer-
cised by the Spirit'.[52] Macchia does not feel that Moltmann's
avoidance of the transcendent as a theological category is sufficient
to meet the criticisms made by pentecostal scholars, or take adequate note of Barth's attempt to hold transcendence and
immanence together.[53] He wants Moltmann to find 'greater value
for this mystery and otherness of God witnessed to among Pentecostals'. For pentecostals this mysterious experience is modelled on
the initial event of Pentecost in Acts. Macchia echoes an earlier criticism of Moltmann that he does not pay sufficient attention to
Luke–Acts but rather focuses on the Pauline epistles. Moltmann

---

[47]   Ibid., 60.
[48]   Moltmann, *Spirit*, 6–7.
[49]   Moltmann, 'Response', 65.
[50]   Ibid.
[51]   Macchia, 'Further Response', 123.
[52]   Ibid., 122.
[53]   Ibid., 123.

suggests that he is doing so to avoid 'enthusiasm that goes beyond the presence of Christ', but Macchia feels this is avoiding the issue.

The question of 'experience' is clearly at the heart of the difference between Moltmann and the pentecostal scholars. Their differing experiences of God lead them to stress either 'transcendence' or 'immanence' without wanting to lose sight of either. The difference here might be summed up thus: Moltmann sees transcendence as experienced through immanence ('immanent transcendence'); pentecostal scholars see immanence as experienced through transcendence. Both want to stress the present experience of God, but Moltmann sees the immanence of God through all life whereas pentecostal scholars see the immanence of God through particular transcendent experiences. In terms of mission this means that Moltmann places the universal experience of life at the heart of mission, whereas pentecostal scholars stress 'signs and wonders' and conversion as central to mission. Land develops the pentecostal outlook in terms of what he calls a 'crisis-development dialectic' that characterises Christian growth.[54] Growth comes through crisis points in which the transcendent activity of God is clearly seen, an idea he links with an understanding of history as 'salvation history'. This can be seen as equivalent to the more popular idea of 'power points' as the means of Christian growth as promoted by John Wimber.[55]

It is notable that the issue of 'signs and wonders' has not featured highly in the debate between evangelicals and ecumenicals mentioned in the previous section. Although in one sense the pentecostal scholars have much in common with evangelicals, they stress the immediate experience of the Spirit in a way that evangelicals do not. This commonality and yet difference is at the heart of the current pentecostal debate over identity. Macchia notes how pentecostals were happy to take much theology over from 'fundamentalists' but only since the 1970s were willing to engage in critical reflection in a way that enabled them to differentiate themselves from evangelicals.[56] More work needs to be done in clarifying

---

[54] Land, *Pentecostal Spirituality*, 117–19.

[55] John Wimber and Kevin Springer, *The Dynamics of Spiritual Growth* (London: Hodder & Stoughton, 1990), 3–7.

[56] Macchia, 'Struggle'.

pentecostal, evangelical and ecumenical identities, perhaps through their different pneumatological understandings and praxis. This would enable a better understanding of the commonalities and differences in mission.

A Developing Framework

In our consideration of the Moltmann–pentecostal debate we have noted a number of issues in the theology of mission. Both Moltmann and the pentecostal scholars share a desire for mission to be holistic in nature and for experience of God to be central to mission. They agree on the need for both the 'particular' and the 'universal' in mission, notably the need for both a church and a creation focus. They also agree on the need for both 'transcendence' and 'immanence' in the experience of mission. However, there is a difference of emphasis and a different sense of movement in the theology of mission of Moltmann and pentecostal scholars. In other words, both Moltmann and pentecostal scholars want to appreciate the variety of blessings that mission involves, but differ in how they see those blessings coming into the life of the church and the world. Moltmann sees the need for a movement from the church to creation, with the work of the Spirit in creation central to his concern. Pentecostal scholars move quickly from a limited view of the future eschatological kingdom to focus on the church (or individuals). In terms of experience, Moltmann stresses the need for what I have called 'transcendence through immanence' whereas pentecostal scholars stress what might be called 'immanence through transcendence'.

These shared concerns and different emphases can be beneficially brought together within the framework of mission being developed through this book. We can see that the basis of this framework is a *polarity* between the particular and the universal.[57] In the context of this chapter polarity can be seen as one primarily

---

[57] This approach has much in common with the dialectical approach to charismatic practical theology outlined by Mark J. Cartledge, *Practical Theology: Charismatic and Empirical Perspectives* (Carlisle: Paternoster Press, 2003), 27–30.

between church and creation. John McIntyre suggests a number of polarities that exist in understanding the Spirit and distinguishes between a polarity and a contradiction: in the latter the two options 'are mutually exclusive and it is logically impossible for any entity to be both at the same time' whereas for a polarity 'while the pure forms of the two members of the antithesis seem to be opposed and negative to one another, in fact they form the foci of what in magnetics would constitute a "field."'[58] The movement between these polarities represent the two movements we identified earlier. This can be represented pictorially as below:

Mission of the Spirit

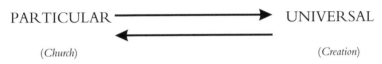

PARTICULAR $\longrightarrow$ UNIVERSAL

(*Church*) (*Creation*)

The Holy Spirit is involved in both the particular and the universal, but it is the Spirit's movement between the two that constitutes mission. This mission of the Spirit involves the church sharing Christ with the whole of creation and people being drawn into the church. It also involves moves to bring experiences of the eschatological kingdom of justice and peace, of healing and joy, into the present-day world and moves by the church to be involved in the political agenda of the world. Such movements represent the 'mission of the Spirit' which people partake in and in doing so get caught up in the *missio Dei*. The task of discernment is crucial to distinguishing what is or is not a valid Christian experience of the Spirit and Yong has much to contribute here.[59] Discernment links with the understanding of blessings and yearnings that has been developed so far. Both form a part of the two movements and sometimes the difference is easy to determine and at other times great discernment is required.

Underlying this framework of mission is the approach to eschatology outlined in the previous chaptert, which gives more detail on

---

[58] John McIntyre, *The Shape of Pneumatology* (Edinburgh: T&T Clark, 1997), 211.
[59] Yong, *Discerning*, 137–48, 243–55.

the movement from the universal to the particular. In considering the particular we need to develop a Christology that embraces the particular – individual faith and communities that grow out of the 'Christ of history' who is encountered in faith today. Adapting the five key pentecostal doctrinal themes identified by Dayton, such a Christology embraces justification, sanctification, healing, second-coming and filling with the Holy Spirit.[60] In the light of Moltmann's work, we need to explore these themes not just in terms of the individual but also in terms of the community and the world. We need to develop an approach that combines pentecostal insights with the outward movement of Moltmann.[61]

Clark Pinnock outlines such a way, if one developed from the biblical rather than theological debate we are considering here. His 'Spirit Christology' begins 'by placing Christology in the context of the Spirit's global operations'.[62] Here is an evangelical approach that values doctrinal themes valued by evangelical and pentecostals and yet seeks to embrace some of Moltmann's concerns. For the purposes of this book I am happy to build on Pinnock's approach and the key relationship between Christ and the Spirit is explored further in the next chapter.

The two movements of the Spirit are essentially experiential and it is important to ask what kind of experiences these movements are characterised by. Our prior discussion suggests that such mission movements are characterised primarily by 'transcendence' or by 'immanence'. In other words, by the 'free critical' working of the Spirit (especially in 'signs and wonders') or the 'life-giving, inductive' working of the Spirit, using the language of the dialogue. Using other language we might understand these as the 'prophetic' or the 'contextual' working of the Spirit in mission. Both are essential to mission and are roughly equivalent to what Bosch calls God's

---

[60] Dayton, *Theological Roots*. Here I am adapting them in the light of the charismatic movement explored earlier in the book. Charismatics are less definitive on a pre-millennial return of Christ and are more hesitant over the term 'baptism in the Spirit'.

[61] For the latter see also Jürgen Moltmann, *The Way of Jesus Christ* (London: SCM, 1990) in which he views Christology from a messianic, eschatological, outlook.

[62] Clark H. Pinnock, *Flame of Love: A Theology of the Holy Spirit* (Downers Grove: InterVarsity Press, 1996), 82.

'no' to the world and God's 'yes' to the world although I am here understanding these pneumatologically.[63] Both are essential to mission and we should be careful not to over-separate these two characteristics of movements in mission. Prophetic movements need to acknowledge God's involvement in creation, otherwise they become irrelevant. Contextual movements need to acknowledge their relationship to the transcendent God, otherwise they can lose their Christian distinctiveness.

In this chapter I have examined the two main ways that the blessings of the Holy Spirit in mission are seen to operate. The charismatic eschatological approach to mission outlined in the previous chapter has been placed within a wider framework for understanding the mission of the Spirit. This framework appears to link well with charismatic experience and is suggestive of a way beyond the evangelical–ecumenical tensions in mission studies. The implications of such an outlook for contextualisation and community are explored in the next two chapters.

---

[63] Bosch, *Transforming Mission*, 10–11.

6

Contextual Mission

> Grace began in 1993 when a small group decided to put on some services that would be different from the usual at their church. The major motivation was an increasing frustration with a church culture that played music that would never be listened to at home, used language that wouldn't be used anywhere else, and a diet that had become over-familiar and often irrelevant. Church had become something 'done to us'. The intention was to seek to worship God in ways and forms that used the cultural resources of the 1990s – the native language of those participating.[1]

It seems natural to assume that the ways we have experienced God in our lives should relate to the way we experience God within church life and worship. But there is often disunity between the two as church culture and our culture differ. Hence, there has been an increasing search by groups such as Grace for 'the native language' to be used in worship. This search links to the mission debate on contextualisation that has been going on for over thirty years. Indeed it can be seen to link right back to the early church in the distinction between converts and proselytes that Walls highlights.[2] Converts turned to Christ with their whole self, including their social, cultural and religious inheritances. They were free to shape their faith and church in line with this turning to Christ that was rooted in their cultural background. This contrasts with the requirement on proselytes that they become 'Jewish' in order to

---

[1] Archbishops' Council, *Mission-Shaped Church*, 45.

[2] Andrew F. Walls, 'Converts or Proselytes? The Crisis over Conversion in the Early Church', *IBMR* 28.1 (2004), 2–7.

become Christian, a requirement that demands a change of culture as well as allegiance. To seek a church of converts is to seek a church ready to be shaped around the whole lives and selfhood of those converts.

The Promise of Contextualisation[3]

We have spoken of the 'contextual' workings of the Spirit and it is now widely recognised that the particularities of Christian faith are always culturally mediated into contexts within creation. It can only be expressed in terms of culture, and has been done so in a variety of ways during the history of Christianity.[4] For many centuries, however, it has been assumed that there was only one orthodox expression of faith, even if different groups held to different understandings of what was orthodox. It was only in the nineteenth century that the influence of culture on theology was recognised, and only in the last century that the influence was examined in detail.[5] The key to greater debate has been the move towards independence seen by many Third World countries through the last century. The term *contextualisation* first appeared in the 1970s in the context of theological education and since then it has become a blanket term for a variety of theological models. Different people prefer different terms, but I prefer to follow Bosch and keep the general term 'contextualisation', which may then be subdivided.[6] The promise of contextualisation is that it allows the gospel to be-

---

[3] An earlier version of the next two sections appeared in Andrew M. Lord, 'The Holy Spirit and Contextualisation', *Asian Journal of Pentecostal Studies* 4.2 (2001), 201–13.

[4] See Walls' examination of six phases of Christian history, *The Missionary Movement in Christian History* (Edinburgh: T&T Clark, 1996), 16–25. Also Aylward Shorter, *Toward a Theology of Inculturation* (New York: Orbis, 1988), 137–63. One definition of culture given by C. Geertz is 'A set of symbols, stories, myths and norms for conduct that orient a society or group cognitively, affectively and behaviourally to the world in which it lives,' quoted in Shorter, *Toward a Theology*, 5. There are other definitions, but this understanding is what is assumed in this article.

[5] Bosch, *Transforming Mission*, 422–3.

[6] Ibid.

come more rooted in particular communities and become more relevant good news for people in different situations. Contextualisation studies add much to an understanding of the 'particular' in mission within the framework I am proposing. However, it is notable that the role of Spirit has received limited treatment in the literature on contextualisation, not being mentioned in the summaries of Bosch or Kirk.[7] For Schreiter the role of the Holy Spirit in the task of contextualisation is not defined, but appears to be one of a background worker of grace in the church: 'One cannot speak of a community developing a local theology without its being filled with the Spirit and working under the power of the gospel.'[8] Bevans mentions the links between the Spirit and life and the African spiritual world understanding in reviewing an example of an anthropological model of contextualisation. He also mentions briefly an inward revelation of the Spirit contributing to transcendental models.[9] But the Spirit is not seen as a central issue in contextualisation. Given the rise of pentecostalism over this same century it is surprising that their experience and reflections have not been drawn into the debate in a significant way. This chapter aims both to develop the model of mission proposed and extend the existing work in contextualisation.

Before we proceed, it is important to note the impact of two Anglican leaders who have contributed to understanding the work of the Spirit in contextualisation: Roland Allen and John V. Taylor. Roland Allen was a high church Anglican missionary in China at the turn of the last century. Writing in the 1920s about the state of mission in the world he concluded, 'We have not yet succeeded in so planting [Christianity] in any heathen land that it has become indigenous.'[10] He saw an answer to this in the missionary methods of St Paul and in a particular emphasis on the work of the Spirit. The doctrine of the Spirit given to all Christians challenges the temptation for missionaries to keep control and so prevent indigenisation. The Spirit gives gifts to all people and guides and directs them in

---

[7] Ibid; Kirk, *Mission*.

[8] Robert J. Schreiter, *Constructing Local Theologies* (New York: Orbis, 1985), 24.

[9] Bevans, *Models*, 54–7, 99.

[10] Roland Allen, *Missionary Methods: St Paul's or Ours?* (Grand Rapids: Eerdmans, 1962), 141.

mission – we need to trust the Spirit in mission.[11] Allen's insights have been very influential in shaping a pentecostal missiology.[12] John V. Taylor, a former leader of CMS, wrote an influential book in the 1970s on the Holy Spirit and mission, *The Go-Between God*. He contended that we cannot separate mission from the work of the Spirit: 'The chief actor in the historic mission of the Christian church is the Holy Spirit. He is the director of the whole enterprise. The mission consists of the things he is doing in the world.'[13] Taylor recognised a divide in contemporary thought between an objective, abstract God and a God seen exclusively through experiences. This divide is similar in some ways to that in the contextualisation debate between church and culture, revelation and experience. Taylor sees this divide overcome when the Holy Spirit becomes central to our thinking. He starts by examining our experience, not of life in general, but of times when we experience something beyond ourselves, the 'numinous'. He calls these moments of 'annunciation', which might be linked with something otherwise quite everyday.[14] These experiences contain a sense of communion between people and God, and this communion is the Holy Spirit, the 'go-between'. The Holy Spirit links us with God and enables communication in both directions. He opens the eyes of people to Christ and so is essential to mission.[15] It is also the Spirit that opens our eyes to other people, enabling us to see them as they uniquely are, and this forms the basis for approaching the task of contextualisation.[16]

To Contextualise or Not?

Pentecostal attitudes to contextualisation differ and in many ways this is one of the most debatable areas in developing a charismatic theology of mission. It is also a key area of debate in understanding

---

[11] Ibid., 142–8.

[12] McGee, 'Missions'.

[13] John V. Taylor, *The Go-Between God: The Holy Spirit and the Christian Mission* (London: SCM, 1972), 5.

[14] Ibid., 8–19.

[15] Ibid., 20.

[16] Here I am developing Taylor's thoughts, ibid., 20. This is in line with his approach in, say, John V. Taylor, *The Primal Vision* (London: SCM, 1963).

pentecostal identity in which the divisions between Western and non-Western pentecostalism can be seen in terms of a reluctance or eagerness to contextualise the gospel.[17] Hollenweger suggests that contextualisation is both the promise and the problem in pentecostal missiology.[18] Here I want to argue that a pentecostal approach to mission will in practice be contextual because of the emphasis on encountering God in particular experiences. Allan Anderson argues that contextual pneumatology is key to pentecostal identity, theology and future, although he acknowledges the need for more work in this area.[19]

We noted earlier that pentecostal missiology is inspired by a literal understanding of the Scriptures with Grant McClung arguing that an emphasis on 'Scripture-Spirit' is the basis for developing a theology of mission.[20] Hence, the dynamic work of the Spirit within the church takes primacy over cultural concerns. Yet one of the first and most influential pentecostals to articulate a theology of mission, Melvin Hodges, focused on indigenous church principles. His emphasis was on gospel and Spirit: 'There is no place on earth where, if the gospel seed be properly planted, it will not produce an indigenous church. The Holy Spirit can work in one country as well as in another.'[21] This is a precursor to Paul Pomerville's 'Spirit translation' model of contextualisation in which there is an unchanged gospel combined with the dynamics of the Holy Spirit. It is the Spirit that produces in individual believers 'unusual zeal and power' that causes them to testify to Christ, provides leadership to the church and enables the church to grow.[22] For Hodges, the focus of the Spirit is within the church, but is directing the church outwards in testimony.

---

[17] For an outline of the debate in relation to AICs, see Anderson, *African Reformation*, 210–14.

[18] Hollenweger, *Pentecostalism*, 298–302.

[19] Anderson, *Pentecostalism*, 14, 198, 283.

[20] McClung Jr, 'Try', 38–40; L. Grant McClung Jr, 'Pentecostal/Charismatic Perspectives on a Missiology for the Twenty-First Century', *PNEUMA* 16 (Spring 1994), 13. See also the approach taken by Pomerville, *Third Force*.

[21] Hodges, *Indigenous Church*, 14.

[22] Ibid., 132.

As the Spirit drives ordinary church members outwards to share the gospel, so the gospel message becomes contextualised. This contextualisation, in part, happens due to the emphasis on experience – linking personal experience and experience of God the Spirit. This contextualisation sometimes contrasts with the official church teaching. Macchia draws a distinction between the abstract doctrinal guides produced by early pentecostal denominations and the contextual preaching. The 'irregular' theology of pentecostal preachers was creative and in touch with everyday experience in contrast to the more abstract doctrinal guides.[23] In the early days it was the experience of 'speaking in tongues' that was seen as the key to contextualisation, enabling witness in the language of people around the world.[24] Experience, enlightened and empowered by the Spirit, is still at the heart of pentecostal missiology.

The danger with this 'irregular' contextualisation is that although it can lead to a theology more in touch with people, it can also lead to cultural misunderstandings and insensitivity, as detailed by Anderson.[25] There is a temptation in not analysing culture to assume that the culture of the preacher is without fault. Harvey Cox sees a tendency for pentecostals to say 'yes' to culture more than they say 'no'.[26] However, perhaps the tendency is rather not to critique the pentecostal community in terms of its cultural influences, and over-critique the 'world' as unduly negative. This is being overcome through a deeper appreciation of social justice issues in pentecostal missiology.[27] McGee suggests that the gift of prophecy has relevance 'to the plight of the poor and [as a] witness against injustice in a world victimized by individual and corporate evils'.[28]

---

[23] Macchia, 'Struggle', 10–11.

[24] Ibid., 17.

[25] Allan Anderson, 'Signs and Blunders: Pentecostal Mission Issues at "Home and Abroad" in the Twentieth Century', *Journal of Asian Mission* 2.2 (2000), 193–210.

[26] Harvey Cox, 'Pentecostalism and Global Market Culture' in Dempster, Klaus and Petersen (eds.), *Globalization of Pentecostalism*, 394–5.

[27] One example of an approach taking social involvement seriously is Douglas Petersen, 'Missions in the Twenty-First Century: Toward a Methodology of Pentecostal Compassion', *Transformation* 16.2 (1999), 54–9.

[28] McGee, 'Pentecostal Missiology', 281.

However, it still seems the case that behind most approaches lies a negative view of culture whereby it brings only social problems to be challenged and overcome through the gospel. This view is supported by a recent survey of European pentecostal-charismatic theologians who perceived a danger in mission of 'uncritically importing specific aspects of the evangelizer's culture to accomplish the task'.[29] Despite this, a number of leaders in the charismatic movement have pointed to the importance of contextualisation, as we saw in Chapter 2.

Contextualisation and Other Faiths[30]

If we allow for a more positive appreciation of contextualisation then the question that faces us is one posed in the last chapter: how do we relate the working of the Spirit in all to the uniqueness of Christ? This question becomes most focused as we consider the relationship between Christian faiths and other faiths. This subject is only just being explored from a pentecostal perspective and is an appropriate way into the subject of how the Spirit and Christ might relate in the particulars of people and churches. The key writers in this area are Clark Pinnock and Amos Yong. Pinnock raises a key question: since most of us allow for God's working in the life of communities outside the church, why do we struggle to accept that God is 'present and makes himself felt … in the religious dimension of cultural life?'[31] Why do we seem to exclude the Spirit from the religious? I think the reason is that we worry about Christ not being proclaimed. Sometimes our concerns here stop us appreciating the work of God outside the Christian faith. The key question for us has to be: how are the ministries of the Holy Spirit and of Jesus Christ

---

[29] Jean-Daniel Plus, 'Globalization of Pentecostalism or Globalization of Individualism? A European Perspective' in Dempster, Klaus and Petersen (eds.), *Globalization of Pentecostalism*, 175. See also McClung's conclusion about the negative encroachment of culture on the church and its mission, McClung Jr, 'Pentecostal/Charismatic Perspectives', 20.

[30] An earlier version of this section first appeared in Andrew M. Lord, 'A Charismatic Approach to Other Faiths', *Asian Journal of Pentecostal Studies* 6.2 (2003).

[31] Pinnock, *Flame of Love*, 200–201.

related? Are they identical? Are they completely independent? A crucial question.

Pinnock, working largely from the biblical material, talks of 'a tension inherent in the Christian faith between universality and particularity' which he relates to 'the twin, independent missions of Son and Spirit'.[32] In these there are the dangers of universalism and restrictivism – 'to say dogmatically that all will be saved … [or] to say that only a few will be'.[33] Pinnock feels that evangelicals are more likely to run into the error of restrictivism and hence need to be challenged towards a more universal understanding of the Spirit. In addition to emphasising the 'Spirit of Christ' we need also to consider the 'Spirit of God'[34] – there is one Spirit who is both tied to Christ and yet free within the Trinity. Much ecumenical work has been done in recent years re-examining the *filioque* clause of the creed which is of vital importance at this point. For Pinnock 'the *filioque* might threaten our understanding of the Spirit's universality'.[35] In attempting to trace the differing roles of Spirit and Christ Pinnock suggests that the Spirit is at work in anyone as they 'open themselves up to love' and receive 'an impression of God's true self'. In doing so the Spirit 'helps inculcate holiness and virtue'. Yet he is quick to say that 'Jesus is *the* criterion of salvation.' The ministries of the Spirit and of Christ are complementary but ultimately a response to Christ is crucial, and in this Pinnock argues that we take our lead from the future eschaton rather than from the present. Whilst agreeing with the need to appreciate the universality of the Spirit, I think it is important not to underplay the particularity of the work of the Spirit in individuals and communities.

Amos Yong feels that Pinnock fails to tackle the question of 'experience' adequately and rushes too fast to a Christological basis for discernment. Yong's concern is to develop a 'metaphysical framework' that will ground a 'pneumatological interpretation of the religions'.[36] His philosophical explorations go beyond our concern here but he wants us to see that every experience is to some degree

---

[32] Ibid., 192.

[33] Ibid., 190.

[34] The greater number of New Testament references to the latter suggests it cannot be ignored.

[35] Pinnock, *Flame of Love*, 196.

[36] Yong, *Discerning*, 98.

one of both word and Spirit and that word and Spirit are 'related but sufficiently distinct' – he uses the image of Irenaeus of the 'two hands of the Father'.[37] There is a certain amount of independence between the Spirit and Christ that is crucial to any positive consideration of other faiths, but these come together under the Father. Drawing on the pentecostal-charismatic tradition and interacting with the work of Harvey Cox, Yong suggests three foundational categories that give a common grounding to a study of religions and also give the basis of pre-Christological categories of discernment. In short, these are religious experience, religious utility and religious cosmology. In discernment we need first to appreciate how the Spirit may be working through the religious experience of someone of another faith; then we must value the ethical change wrought by this experience on the person by the Spirit; and finally we must understand the theological and soteriological meaning of the experience. Practically speaking, Yong is trying to get us to pause and appreciate others before we rush in with Christ.

Yong's most significant contribution, I think, is to outline a philosophical basis for the distinct yet linked roles of the Spirit and Christ in our experience. In this he builds particularly on the work of C.S. Pierce and Donald Gelpi. For Yong 'all experience can be understood as mediatedness and is, theologically, essentially of the Spirit'.[38] The religious dimension of experience is characterised by 'heightened sense of truth, beauty, excellence, goodness and reality as it was and is meant to be'. The Spirit is seen:

> as the divine power who constitutes the manyness of world, each in its own authenticity and integrity, and who unites the manyness of the world in harmony. Insofar as the Spirit is present and at work, the norms, ideals and values of each thing will be fulfilled. In this sense, it is possible to understand the mission of the Spirit as distinct from that of the Word. Eschatologically, of course, there will be a convergence of Spirit and Word in the full revelation of the divine mystery.[39]

Hence, it is also possible for Yong to say that word and Spirit 'are *both* present universally and particularly in creation … however, the

---

[37] Yong, *Beyond the Impasse*, 26.
[38] Yong, *Discerning*, 122.
[39] Ibid., 132.

dimensions of universality and particularity differ for each'.[40] In a sense the work of the Spirit is to bring each thing to its integrity (to be what they were created to be) and where there is an absence of the Spirit we see a lack of integrity and creativity. The ultimate integrity can of course be seen in Christ and in this sense the Spirit cannot be seen separate from Christ.[41] This understanding has much in common with the approaches of Moltmann and others outlined earlier, although surprisingly Yong does not interact at any length with such scholars.

Having allowed a greater role for the Spirit, the question of discernment comes to the fore. If the Spirit is only seen under Christ then discernment is much easier – all who reject Christ reject the Spirit. When we allow for the Spirit's working even where Christ may not be named we have to be more careful, particularly when considering the religious sphere. Hence, Pinnock and Yong, and indeed Moltmann, end up stressing the need for discernment and proposing appropriate categories for this task. The question is: what characterises the work of the Spirit? This is complicated by an acknowledgement of the working of the Spirit in the whole of life, individual, communal and political, life-giving and demonic: 'A robust sense of discernment is therefore needed so as to be able to engage the various dimensions of human experience in all of their interconnectedness and complexity.'[42] In this task Yong outlines two approaches: one based on the broad categories of divine presence, absence and activity;[43] and one based on the foundational categories that is more appropriate to a consideration of other faiths.[44] He gives a very thorough and penetrating approach to Christian discernment which will repay further study.

If Yong's strengths lie in his philosophical engagement and his holistic and detailed approach to discernment, then his weaknesses are perhaps more in the realm of personhood and eschatology. Although Yong desires to maintain the personal nature of the Holy Spirit and possible personal interpretations of 'spirits' he stresses the working of the Spirit in all things in a way that is hard to conceive of

---

[40] Ibid., 116.

[41] Ibid., 179.

[42] Yong, *Beyond the Impasse*, 165.

[43] Ibid.

[44] Yong, *Discerning*, ch. 7.

in personal terms. The move away from understanding the Spirit as the 'bond of love' between Father and Son, as in Augustine,[45] whilst gaining much in terms of the working of the Spirit in the world has lost an immediate personal context for the Spirit. Moltmann starts from a similar perspective to Yong and although he lacks the philosophical precision he does wrestle rather better in understanding the Spirit by means of the personal as well as impersonal metaphors in Scripture.[46] But the pentecostal scholar Chan does not feel Moltmann gives a personal enough account and his criticisms could also be aimed at Yong.[47] In terms of approaching other faiths, the lack of a more personal understanding of the Holy Spirit tends to mean that Yong's approach lacks an emphasis on the people of other faiths – these seem secondary, rather than primary as has been often argued.[48] He does address questions surrounding mediums in the Umbandist tradition but his interpretation of the spiritual forces involved is more impersonal than personal (in contrast to the views of the mediums themselves).[49] The question of the personal can also be raised in terms of community, the body of persons. Yong appears to reduce the importance of community in discernment and does not consider at any length the relationship between the church and communities of other faiths. If the Spirit is at work in all things then how do we define the uniqueness of the Spirit within the Christian community? There are a number of issues here where further thought is required in developing Yong's approach.

One of the other points of contention in a dialogue between Moltmann and pentecostal scholars was the difference between the 'life-giving' work of the Spirit in bringing life and the 'free-critical' work of the Spirit in challenging current experience.[50] How the work of the Spirit finds a foundation in eschatology as well as in creation is a key issue. Yong prefers to talk of sacrament rather than eschatology in his understanding of Pentecost, although he does

---

[45] Veli-Matti Kärkkäinen, *Pneumatology: The Holy Spirit in Ecumenical, International, and Contextual Perspective* (Grand Rapids: Baker, 2002), 46–8.

[46] Moltmann, *Spirit*, 268–88.

[47] Chan, 'Asian', 39.

[48] E.g. by Andrew Wingate, *Encounter in the Spirit: Muslim–Christian Dialogue in Practice* (Geneva: WCC, 1988).

[49] Yong, *Discerning*, 273–5.

[50] Lord, 'Moltmann-Pentecostal Dialogue'.

make brief mention of the Spirit as 'usher in the new creation'.[51] In a more recent book Yong expands on this, but his concern is more for the universal workings of the Spirit in all creation than in considering the different kinds of working of the Spirit.[52] These thoughts are in need of further development and interaction with the wider pentecostal understandings of Pentecost and eschatology. Without this it is difficult to address the question of 'conversion' and the prophetic aspects of mission, where sometimes Christians find themselves working alongside those of other faiths. In terms of conversion, Yong is trying to overcome the reliance of Gelpi's philosophy on conversion and to balance the evangelical stress on transformation with an appreciation of other people in dialogue. He has not yet devoted himself to the subject of salvation and conversion in any depth, but perhaps hints that this may relate to the criteria of discernment focus on Jesus in support of a more exclusivist position.[53] We wait with some expectancy these developments in Yong's thinking and we must take care of making judgments ahead of time.

Developing the Framework of Mission

Returning to the framework our discussion has given more detail to the movement of the Spirit from the particular to the universal. It is within this movement that it is easiest to stress either Christology or pneumatology and is hardest to hold both together. In terms of other faiths this can be seen in some 'exclusivist' or 'pluralist' positions that can stress one at the expense of the other. I have suggested that pentecostal approaches to mission are inherently contextual and must bring together Christology and pneumatology. Developing some of the thoughts of Amos Yong I have suggested what might form the basis of such an approach that fits with the framework I am developing. This basis can be expressed in terms of the following principles:

---

[51] Yong, *Discerning*, 167.
[52] Yong, *Beyond the Impasse*, 35–42.
[53] Ibid., 127–8.

Universal: (u1) everything in creation is *influenced* by the
                     Holy Spirit.
                (u2) everything in creation is *challenged* by the
                     Holy Spirit.
Particular: (p1) the Holy Spirit is *personal*.
                (p2) this influence and challenge is shaped around
                     Jesus Christ.
                (p3) the *intensity* of the Holy Spirit relates to the
                     response to God.

The foundational pneumatology of Yong provides a solid basis for
seeing the work of the Holy Spirit as influencing all of creation (u1).
But his understanding of the work of the Spirit needs to be nuanced
through a differentiation between the 'life-giving' and the 'critical'
work which will better highlight the importance of challenge (u2). I
have already commented on the need for the Holy Spirit to be seen
in personal terms. As we see in Acts, the working of the Spirit is so
often particular, personal and recognisable (p1). This working is
shaped around the person of Jesus Christ who is preached and to
whom people are drawn (p2). The personal and relational working
of the Spirit around Christ leads to the formation of the church as
the community of Christ. There is a sense here that the response of
people to God indicates that there exist different 'intensities' of the
Spirit – there is a general intensity of the Spirit's working in the
world, and a particular more intense working of the Spirit seen in
the response of people to Christ (p3). This intense working is linked
to personal response and to a greater Spirit–Christ overlap in terms
of their working. Yong hints at this in his eschatology in which the
future creation is marked by a greater overlap (equality?) between
the workings of the Spirit and Christ.

   In thinking about the meaning of mission in the context of other
faiths we need to go beyond the idea of individuals sharing 'the gospel' with others, vital though this is. Within my framework
Christians are caught up in a movement of the Holy Spirit who is
ever drawing us out of our personal and communal experience of
God in Christ towards the world and the whole creation which
we are called to influence and challenge. As we get caught in this
movement we realise that the Spirit is already at work, in creation
and in those of other faiths, and so we find ourselves in a movement

alongside others as the Spirit leads. This is not to deny our particular experience of the Spirit centred around Christ but rather to say that this cannot exclude other workings of the Spirit in people and creation. This movement is, for us, one in the Spirit with Christ and one in which we cannot but share through our whole lives the reality of Christ. Yet it is more than evangelism, for we may be moved alongside others of all faiths or none in social action, in protest for justice, in environmental concern. Such holistic mission, as part of a wider movement of the eschatological Spirit, cannot but result in a deepening Spirit–Christ overlap by which others see more of Christ. Response to Christ does determine final individual salvation but this is not to say that those who don't respond can't be caught up in a movement of the Spirit now that brings in more of God's kingdom and gives them a greater reality of Christ to respond to.

7

Community Mission

Anne had a visionary and prophetic ministry ... She felt that a community of shared lives would deepen the sense of community through the whole church ... We had the obvious model of the early church who had 'all things in common' ... and the strength and credibility of their witness lay largely in the quality of their corporate life together. 'See how these Christians love one another!' was the cry of the pagan observer.[1]

So began the creation of extended households in St Michael-le-Belfrey in York during the 1970s. These were experiments that lasted over five years and were formative in the ministry of those involved. Although the households didn't last and suffered many strains, they have shaped the community-based outlook of many charismatic leaders. So far in our considerations we have left aside the issue of community and we must now consider its importance in mission, allowing for different practical ways in which such communities can be realised. Over the last century one of the most important rediscoveries in mission was that 'it is the *community* that is the primary bearer of mission'.[2] Michael McCoy has recently developed Bosch's insights to suggest that 'community *in its own right*' can be seen 'as a new or emerging paradigm of mission for a postmodern world'.[3] I will return to the question of whether the local church community can bear the full weight of God's mission

[1] Watson, *You are my God*, 114.

[2] Bosch, *Transforming Mission*, 472.

[3] Michael McCoy, '"Community": A Postmodern Mission Paradigm?', *Journal of Anglican Studies* 1.1 (2003), 32.

later, but we cannot avoid an emphasis on community unless we are willing to surrender to an individualistic understanding of mission. The framework of mission that I have been developing needs extending to recognise that the movements of the Spirit are essentially community movements rather than movements of individuals, although the latter interpretation must be left as a possibility.

There are many possible definitions of 'community' and here I am assuming a general sociological definition that sees community as 'a number of people who interact with each other on a regular basis'.[4] These interactions form groups with distinct social identities and behaviour. Christian communities will have their identities and behaviour shaped by the story of Jesus Christ and the Trinitarian nature of God.[5] My interest here is to consider how Christian communities are central to the mission of the Spirit. I want to suggest that a useful way forward is by considering the 'voluntary principle' that within the missionary movement brings together mission, community and the work of the Spirit. In brief, my argument is that when the Spirit breaks into our experience we will naturally find ourselves drawn together with others who share something in the Spirit. The communities that are formed are God's vehicle for mission and will constantly find themselves driven by the Spirit into the world. This combines both movements of the Spirit that are a part of my framework for mission. We can therefore see how communities are an essential part of God's blessings in mission. These communities will be of diverse nature and some will overlap geographically or within denominations or church traditions, whereas others will be seen as completely distinct. The tensions that come from this perhaps remind us that communities always come with yearnings: for unity, for structures that bring life, for ways of working together for God's kingdom. This chapter explores some of these themes and is suggestive of what a charismatic ecclesiology might look like. The aim is not to develop a full-blown ecclesiology but rather to explore the more particular link between the Spirit, community and mission.

---

[4] Anthony Giddens, *Sociology* (Cambridge: Polity Press, 1993), 285–6.
[5] For more details on this in a different context see Andrew M. Lord, 'Virtual Communities and Mission', *Evangelical Review of Theology* 26.3 (2002), 197–8.

Pentecostal-Charismatic Mission Communities

As we noted in Chapter 2, pentecostal ecclesiology has tended to focus on individual assemblies or congregations. This focus can positively generate communities that are attractive in mission, drawing others into faith. Charismatic approaches within the historic church traditions stress the blessings the Spirit brings to local Christian communities, for example renewal (Michael Harper), reflections of the Trinity (Tom Smail) and celebration (Jean-Jacques Suurmond).[6] There is much to appreciate here about the blessings of the Spirit that make Christian communities attractive in mission, picking up on characteristics (6) and (7) we noted in Chapter 4. Steven Land develops these in terms of 'missionary fellowships' based around the affections of gratitude, compassion and courage.[7] However, alone, this focus on local Christian communities can become very inward looking and undermine the work of mission. Hence, there is also a stress on church being the place where people are sent in mission by the Spirit. The Great Commission and the impending kingdom have sent many people out of communities to share the good news with the world. I want to suggest that although this is valuable we need to see the Spirit as both the *former* as well as the *sender* of communities in mission. Otherwise we fall into the trap of seeing mission as independent of communities and church. I will go on to argue that we need to see the Spirit as the *uniter* of communities if we are to avoid the divisions and disputes that continue to plague the work of mission.

Pinnock's work is a useful starting point. The sending image he develops has great vitality and life: 'The church rides the wind of God's Spirit like a hawk endlessly and effortlessly circling and gliding in the summer sky. It ever pauses to wait for impulses of power to carry it forward to the nations.'[8] He then goes on to make the point that 'Christ did not first establish the church and add the Spirit secondarily ... the church is born and empowered by the Spirit.'[9] The birth and empowering of the church by the Spirit is directed at

---

[6] Jean-Jacques Suurmond, *Word and Spirit at Play: Towards a Charismatic Theology* (London: SCM Press, 1994).

[7] Land, *Pentecostal Spirituality*, ch. 3.

[8] Pinnock, *Flame of Love*, 114.

[9] Ibid., 115.

the transformation of the world. In the language of this book the Spirit moves to bring to birth particular Christian communities that continually ride the wind of the Spirit as they are directed outwards evermore universally into the world. This ride embraces both the blessings of creation and the suffering love of Christ as the church yearns for the kingdom of God.[10] Pinnock provides a helpful basis for a charismatic ecclesiology which I want to develop through a greater exploration of the ways mission communities are born and the ways they work together, themes that are marginal to Pinnock's discussion.

Voluntary Communities[11]

A useful way into considering how the Spirit brings to birth Christian communities is through an examination of the 'voluntary principle' which brings together community, mission and the Spirit. In this section I outline the idea as it was found in the missionary movement in order to illustrate its importance. In the following section I develop the principle on the basis of pentecostal experience.

There are two difficulties to face when thinking about the voluntary principle. First, there has been surprisingly little study of the subject.[12] Secondly, the little that has been done has focused on praxis, on how the principle was worked out in voluntary societies.[13] Facing the latter problem I want to suggest that although an

---

[10] 'The church is the instrument of Christ, called to carry on his mission in the power of the Spirit. This power is a special kind of power, since he who baptizes us in the Spirit is the Lamb and Servant of God (Jn 1:29, 33). This means paradoxically that though it is the power of creation, it is also the power of suffering love, which does not remove our weakness or eliminate pain.' Ibid., 116.

[11] Earlier versions of the following two sections can be found in Andrew M. Lord, 'The Voluntary Principle in Pentecostal Missiology', *Journal of Pentecostal Theology* 17 (2000), 81–95. In the earlier work I neglected to consider explicitly the community dimension of the voluntary principle even though it is key to the praxis.

[12] Walls, *The Missionary Movement*, 241.

[13] Walls suggests that 'There never was a *theology* of the voluntary society.' Ibid., 246.

underlying voluntary principle was key, it was initially only perceived through its outworkings through voluntary societies. It was
only much later, as a result of controversies this century, that the
principle was articulated with more theological precision. This separation of the principle from the outworkings is consistent with
William Carey's distinction between prayer (the principle) and
'means', which Andrew Walls identifies as the key development
leading to the development of voluntary societies.[14]

The voluntary principle can be defined as follows:

> It is the Holy Spirit, working in the hearts of individual be-
> lievers, that brings them together for the work of Christian
> mission.

Below are four practical implications that help clarify our understanding of the principle.

Implications:

(1)   Mission is primarily motivated without reference to
      church organisations, i.e. mission is primarily a
      'bottom-up' not a 'top-down' activity.
(2)   Mission is the domain of every believer, i.e. not
      limited to a particular class of person, e.g. clergy,
      religious.
(3)   Mission arises out of experiences of God, i.e. more
      than out of just human concern or cultural context.
(4)   Mission flows from communities rather than
      individuals.

This definition needs examining within the history of the missionary movement. To focus the study I will examine the voluntary
principle within the general historical survey of Walls[15] and in the
particular context of CMS. The CMS is one of the earliest Anglican
missionary societies, founded in 1799, which has contributed
greatly to the spread of the church in Africa and elsewhere.

Starting with the practical implications, it is difficult today
to appreciate the impact the voluntary principle had on mission
in the church. Walls talks of it 'influencing, supplementing, and

---

[14]   Ibid., 242–6.
[15]   Ibid., 241–54.

by-passing the life of Church and State alike'.[16] During the eigh-
teenth century most people thought in terms only of a parish church
or of a congregation. That mission could arise out of a community
of people called by God without primary reference to the church
structures was radical, particularly as people had given themselves
in previous centuries in defence of particular forms of church
government. It also raised the status of lay people, hence the second
implication. Lay people could become leaders in missionary societies with more influence than clergy. Missionary societies were also
dependent upon lay inspiration – it was local associations of people
that transformed the CMS in the early 1800s, enabling greater
mission.[17]

In part it was a prompting from God, particularly through
preaching, that challenged people to ask 'What shall we do?' and led
them to seek something beyond what the church was then offering.
It was out of group prayer meetings that voluntary associations
grew.[18] The importance of an experience of God grew with the development of 'faith missions' in the late nineteenth century, which
represented 'a development of the voluntary society rather than a
totally new departure'.[19] Mission was often seen in the practical experience and provision of God. Although missionary societies were
largely evangelistic, other voluntary societies took up wider social
issues. This points to the importance of the wider social context of
the time: 'The voluntary society, and its special form in the missionary society, arose in a particular period of Western social, political,
and economic development and was shaped by that period.'[20] It
could not, Walls argues, have developed in a dictatorship or in a situation of poverty. However, I would want to argue that separating
out the voluntary from its practical implications at the time allows
for appropriate outworkings in other political and economic situations. In this work I am developing a more modern understanding
of Christian community rather than use the terms 'society' or 'association' that are set within a past historical context.

---

[16] Ibid., 241.
[17] Ibid., 250–51.
[18] Ibid., 242–6.
[19] Ibid., 252.
[20] Ibid., 253.

The definition of the voluntary principle came into focus for CMS particularly through two controversies of the last century and through the work and thinking of Max Warren, former CMS General Secretary. Firstly, there was the view that the church should be its own missionary society, not requiring any separate society. In contrast Warren argued that 'Historical evidence showed that [missionary societies] had emerged at times of spiritual *revival*, that they owed much to *lay* initiative and that always the *personal* emphasis in their structures and operations had been uppermost.'[21] It is clear that not every member of every church is committed to mission and a committed community and hence a *spiritual vanguard* is needed.[22] The second controversy surrounded the integration of the International Missionary Council (IMC) into the World Council of Churches. The IMC had been largely composed of mission society representatives and it was hoped that by integrating it into a united church more mission would be achieved. Warren argued that 'Mission has, in fact, as often as not, been an activity posing acute challenges to the pursuit of organisational unity'[23] and that 'organs of voluntary action must exist if there is to be spiritual experimentation and initiative'.[24] In these arguments Warren argues in line with our four implications. The key theological issues for Warren were those of the Holy Spirit and the laity. In 1957 Warren set forth a vision for the CMS, *Towards 1999*, in which he argues that the theological principles involved in voluntary associations derive:

> from the doctrine of the Holy Spirit which sees him as ever seeking fresh initiatives in the life of [hu]mankind, and never confining himself or his activities to the institutional life of the Church. This further carries with it a high doctrine of the laity which sees the ordinary man and woman as being always potential means by which the Holy Spirit takes some of his initiatives.[25]

---

[21] F.W. Dillistone, *Into All the World: A Biography of Max Warren* (London: Hodder & Stoughton, 1980), 114.

[22] Max Warren, *Crowded Canvas: Some Experiences of a Life-Time* (London: Hodder & Stoughton, 1974), 158.

[23] Quoted in Dillistone, *Into All the World*, 121.

[24] Warren, *Crowded Canvas*, 157.

[25] Quoted in Dillistone, *Into All the World*, 116.

These arguments were to be taken up by succeeding CMS General Secretaries John V. Taylor and Simon Barrington-Ward, both theologians of the Spirit.[26] The current General Secretary, Tim Dakin, is seeking to develop Taylor's understanding of the Holy Spirit to develop a contemporary understanding of the voluntary, missional church.[27] Whilst my approach has much in common with that of Dakin, I want to draw more explicitly on the pentecostal contribution.

Charismatic Mission Communities

The above historical sketch illustrates how mission, community and the Spirit come together as we emphasise the voluntary principle in our thinking about the church. It will be obvious from our earlier discussions that the implications of the principle are also key to pentecostal mission. This is not surprising given the historical links between the missionary and pentecostal movements. The voluntary association was common in the nineteenth century Holiness movement out of which the pentecostal movement came. Such associations enabled people to be particularly involved in social reform and to come together for Bible study, testimony and prayer.[28] Early pentecostals also gained inspiration from 'faith missions' through the influence of A.B. Simpson and hence, I suggest, taking on board some of the ideas of the voluntary principle.[29] But perhaps the most significant overlap between the two movements is the desire for world evangelisation that embraced similar methods as well as aims.

We need to avoid the tendency to suggest that some of the characteristics of pentecostal mission are unique to that movement

---

[26] Consider John V. Taylor's reflections on the Spirit as the 'go-between' initiator of mission, *The Go-Between God*, and Simon Barrington-Ward's comment that missionary movements 'have been spontaneous up-rushings of the life of the Spirit', *Love Will Out* (Basingstoke: Marshall, Morgan & Scott, 1988), 183.

[27] Tim Dakin, 'Communion in Mission', *CMS Newsletter* 553 (2002), 2–23.

[28] Faupel, *Everlasting Gospel*, 52, 61–3.

[29] McGee, 'Missions', 620.

when they have been present before in the missionary, and other, movements. For example, experiences of God have motivated mission in the past,[30] lay people have been mobilised in mission prior to the last century, and previous mission was not all linked with bureaucratic organisations.[31] Expanding the list of implications (p. 108), it is, however, important to note some of the developments that are relevant to our concerns here:

(5)   Experiences of God form links with primal religion and importantly include 'signs and wonders'.

(6)   Mission brings together those on 'the margins' as well as the prosperous and powerful.

(7)   Mission involves the formation of indigenous Christian communities, rather than communities characterised by foreign cultural practices.

The pentecostal experience of God has clear links with primal religion in a way that was not the case in the missionary movement. The missionary movement as a whole was not sympathetic to their converts' previously held primal religions and it is only this century that the study of such religions has become important.[32] This is perhaps most clearly seen in indigenous pentecostal churches such as those in Latin America, which connect with the local folk religion in a way very different from the Christianity of North American missionaries.[33] It is also commented on by North American pentecostals such as Paul Pomerville, who talks about the value of pentecostal experience to the conversion of the 'non-Christian animistic-oriented peoples of the Third World'.[34] Harvey Cox

---

[30]   Bonino suggests that all 'great missionary thrusts are associated with renewals in spirituality'. José Míguez Bonino, 'Pentecostal Mission is More than what it Claims', *PNEUMA* 16.2 (1994), 283.

[31]   Here Gerloff overstates her case on the importance of black organisation to the development of pentecostalism by characterising all Western denominations as being centralised and bureaucratic. Roswith Gerloff, 'Pentecostals in the African Diaspora' in Anderson and Hollenweger (eds.), *Pentecostals After a Century*, MS.48.

[32]   See Walls, *The Missionary Movement*, 119–39 for a review of the development of such study.

[33]   Karl-Wilhelm Westmeier, 'Themes of Pentecostal Expansion in Latin America', *International Bulletin of Missionary Research* (April 1993), 76.

[34]   Pomerville, *Third Force*, 104. This is a generalised and rather condescending phrase, perhaps a grudging admission of the point.

speaks of pentecostalism as a kind of primal spirituality which brings to the surface modes of worship that have been submerged by centuries of Western Christian moralism and rationality.[35] Although Cox perhaps overstates his case, it seems clear that the pentecostal experience of God is linked in a deeper way with people's underlying hopes, longings and motivations than was the case in the earlier missionary movement. Looking in more detail at the pentecostal experiences of God, they were clearly more varied than in the missionary movement. 'One can hardly open a book of pentecostal reminiscences from the vertiginous years that followed the Azusa Street revival without signs and wonders tumbling out of the pages.'[36] Although William Faupel does trace such pentecostal experiences back to the revival movements of the nineteenth century and before, they do not dominate the missionary movement as they do the spread of pentecostalism.[37]

The missionary movement made missionaries and significant leaders out of many lay people. But the movement grew from amongst the economically more prosperous Western nations of the time. In contrast, pentecostalism was born amongst those on the margins, the disinherited: 'The pentecostal movement ... erupted from among society's disenfranchised, and it envisioned a human community restored by the power of the Spirit.'[38] From this start we have now reached a point where missionaries from the Third World are increasing at a decadal growth rate of 248 per cent, 5 times the growth rate of Western missions.[39] This represents a significant change in mission patterns and thus, I suggest, pentecostal mission has extended the notion of every believer beyond the economically rich to include those on the margins. This validates my earlier assertion that the voluntary principle can be separated from its immediate economic and social context. We have noted that the development of indigenous churches has been central to pentecostal missiology in a way uncommon within the earlier missionary movement. The missionary movement laid the basis for indigenous

---

[35] Cox, *Fire from Heaven*, 101.

[36] Ibid., 69.

[37] The difference is perhaps in the variety and quantity of experiences of the Spirit seen in pentecostalism as opposed to the missionary movement.

[38] Cox, *Fire from Heaven*, 24.

[39] Hollenweger, *Pentecostalism*, 288.

churches in the 'Three Self Principles' articulated by Henry Venn,[40] but these were not well applied at the time.[41] The pentecostal movement brought the life that the principles needed in order for them to become widely adopted at the heart of missionary praxis.[42] Indigenous churches are by definition grown 'bottom-up', not controlled by a distant church or mission centre. As such they place greater value on lay people and on the shared community culture.[43] Walls identifies prophetic revelation which, following Cox, may be due to a closer link between indigenous churches and the prior primal religious traditions.[44] Thus there appears a clear link between the development of indigenous churches and the voluntary principle, although more work is needed to explore this link further.

The seven characteristics of 'voluntary communities' can be brought together within my suggested model to give essential practical characteristics of any charismatic mission community:

(a) Reliance on the guiding and empowering of the Holy Spirit both to form communities and send them forever outwards into the world in holistic mission.

(b) Seeking encounters with God: both of 'signs and wonders' and encounters that connect with people's underlying hopes and longings.

(c) Promoting every-member mission.[45]

---

[40] The establishment of self-supporting, self-governing and self-propagating churches.

[41] Bosch, *Transforming Mission*, 307ff.

[42] The principles were mediated to early pentecostal missionaries through A.B. Simpson's training college at Nyack. See McGee, 'Missions', 620.

[43] Anderson links the rapid formation of indigenous churches to the experience of Spirit-baptism which empowers all, breaking down any divide between 'clergy' and 'laity'. See Anderson, 'Global Pentecostalism', MS.169.

[44] Walls, *The Missionary Movement*, 116, although Walls does not develop the links between AICs and primal religious traditions. Cox links the prophetic, together with other forms of 'primal piety' as they occur in pentecostalism, with the influence of primal African spirituality, *Fire from Heaven*, 101.

[45] I owe this term to Tim Dakin, 'Mission Out of Order', *CMS Newsletter* 551 (2001), 5–7.

(d)   Seeing mission as something done together and not
      alone.
(e)   Developing a 'mixed' community of different people.[46]
(f)   Grounding the community in the surrounding culture.

This provides a useful agenda for any Christian community to eval-
uate itself against, applicable to church congregations, cells, home
groups, prayer groups, workplace groups, denominational committees – whatever. They can be summarised under the headings
'Prayer' (a)–(b), 'Action' (c), 'Togetherness' (d)–(e) and 'Connect-
edness' (f). Charismatic communities have traditionally tended to
focus on the first two and are in need of developing the latter two.

Communities and Structures

Perhaps the greatest dangers to mission communities are the temptations to over-organise God rather than rely on his Spirit. Within
pentecostalism the fairly spontaneous expansion of the movement
has been replaced in some circles by an emphasis on church growth
strategy. Pomerville goes as far as to suggest that 'Pentecostals also
could be characterized as having a church growth oriented mission
strategy.'[47] This can be backed up by Cox's observations about the
highly organised Korean evangelist campaign 'Here's Life Korea'
and Johnson's list of the ninety-nine pentecostal/charismatic global
plans for world evangelisation this century.[48] Yet some structures
and organisations are required and in this section we explore further
the work of the Holy Spirit as *uniter* already in evidence in (d)–(e)
above. In the early pentecostal movement, 'Speaking in unknown
tongues represented a point when all distinctions, race, class, gen-
der, would enrich rather than divide.'[49] Tongues spoke of an

---

[46] A 'fellowship of the unlike', to use the phrase of Simon Barrington-
Ward.

[47] Pomerville, *Third Force*, 109.

[48] Cox, *Fire from Heaven*, 232; Todd M. Johnson, 'Global Plans in the
Pentecostal/Charismatic Tradition and the Challenge of the Unevangelized World' in Jan A.B. Jongeneel (ed.), *Pentecost, Mission and Ecumenism* (Frankfurt: Peter Lang, 1992).

[49] Faupel, *Everlasting Gospel*, 198, referring to the outlook of Seymour.

essential unity seen in the way that people of all races and back-
grounds praise God together. It is important to recognise the
yearning of the Spirit for unity and I want to suggest here that the
Holy Spirit works to unite by the creation of partnerships and as the
'go-between' brings mission communities together within the
movement out into the world.

Before developing this further it is important to step back and acknowledge three of the criticisms often levelled at voluntary
groups. Perhaps most critically, a focus on voluntary communities
can mean that individuals abdicate their responsibility for mission.
The task of mission is assigned to particular communities, perhaps
mission societies and organisations, which only those keen on mission join in with. Secondly, the existence of such communities
independent of denominational structures can mean that structural
mission is ignored: it is the local communities rather than, say, bish-
ops and dioceses that are involved in mission. This has caused
problems when churches are planted in other cultures – some of the
churches planted have lacked a structural mission impetus and become over-reliant on outside mission societies. Thirdly, following
on from the last point, voluntary mission communities have often
assumed the existence of territorial church structures that would
provide nurture and order. This is an issue Tim Dakin feels strongly
about and argues that in the culture of today we need to go beyond
the territorial approach found in the Anglican church in terms of di-
ocesan and parish orders.

These are valid criticisms of voluntary mission communities as
they flourished within the missionary movement. Dakin's solution
is first of all to build on the work of Wolfgang Simson and Avery
Dulles to 'suggest that the *community of disciples* might offer an attractive, integrating model for our time … pointing towards a visible
church whose character resembles voluntary mission movements'.[50]
The most rooted approach to voluntary mission communities, he
suggests, 'which offers "the least possible withdrawal" [from the
world] is that of the *little congregations*, what are to be normative'.[51]
Here we have a theological framework that could be used to support the cell church approach to church order and growth.[52] To

---

[50] Dakin, 'Communion in Mission', 4.
[51] Ibid., 10.
[52] An approach pioneered by Ralph Neighbour.

overcome the third criticism these 'little communities' are to be linked in a flexible way to each other within the unity of the Spirit's evangelistic action: 'The fundamental proposal is that the church should be understood as a communion in mission – a fellowship of the Holy Spirit oriented towards mission in the world. The focus for communion is not centred in denominational structures (as instruments of unity) but in the mystery of the Spirit's evangelistic presence.'[53] Dakin proposes a Spirit-based rather than structural approach to unity that hopes to overcome the territorial approaches of the past. This approach also overcomes the first criticism in that it becomes normative for *all* Christians to be members of 'little communities' and hence to be aware of their part in God's mission.

But we are still left with the question of structures – a Spirit-based approach still requires visible structures if communion is to mean anything and these structures must have mission at their heart to overcome the second criticism above. Dakin addresses at length the Anglican concepts of communion concluding with a suggested 'fellowship' model of communion whereby an Anglican is 'someone who is in fellowship with a bishop who is in fellowship with Canterbury'.[54] It is not completely clear how such a fellowship structure fits alongside the existence of voluntary mission agencies. I want to acknowledge and commend much of Dakin's underlying theology, unsurprisingly perhaps, given our common emphasis on the voluntary principle. But I want to suggest that we tackle the structural issues in a slightly different way. Like Dakin, I want to emphasise the importance of charismatic mission communities and have defined these in a way that emphasises their birth, character and growth in the Spirit as they are taken ever deeper into the world. But there are four issues that Dakin does not address as fully as he might: the inherent sinfulness of communities – not all small communities will be mission communities; the need for mid-level structures – communities may well group with others nearby; some focus on territory is necessary for contextualisation, so we cannot dismiss the territorial nature of Christianity;[55] communities

---

[53] Dakin, 'Communion in Mission', 2.

[54] Ibid., 22.

[55] In this regard a stimulating argument for the importance of place to Christian life and mission is given by John Inge, *A Christian Theology of Place* (Aldershot: Ashgate, 2003).

often overlap – people may belong to more than one mission community. Rather than develop the dialogue with Dakin within the Anglican scene I want here to suggest a broader approach based on the Spirit's yearning for unity.

In any Christian church structure there will be a variety of communities and sub-communities linked together in different ways. These may be leadership teams, cell groups, area leaders' meetings, elders' groups, finance committees, world mission teams, Alpha groups, building development teams, and so on. Their formation in the Spirit will mean that these are brought together through a shared character, function and desire for partnership. Dakin speaks of a shared fellowship based on a 'shared vision and values'.[56] Within the approach I have been developing this is fulfilled in a shared vision for holistic mission (Chapter 4) and the core values of charismatic mission communities (a)–(f). When these are held by all communities, whatever their function, then the church as a whole is energised in new ways for mission. Despite their particular different functions such communities share the general function of the Spirit, in whom they are immersed, to experience the yearnings of the world and share the blessings of God in Christ with the world. Such shared vision, values and function is sufficient to provide a unity in terms of participation in the Spirit's mission. Within particular denominations and church traditions these will be shaped by histories and personalities that give different foci to what is held in common, as we might expect given the contextual work of the Spirit through experience and history. Here I am suggesting a shape 'from above' for the structures of a church based on a shape explored 'from below' for small charismatic mission communities. This is one way of balancing the demands of 'structure' and 'communitas' that Vincent Turner identified and which has been a point of reflection within the missionary movement.[57]

A key point in the approach here is that mission communities see the need for working in partnership with others, developing characteristics (d) and (e) above. A purely congregational or cell-based approach is not, I want to suggest, sufficient if the church is to enter into the fullness of the Spirit's mission. Small local communities

---

[56] Dakin, 'Communion in Mission', 21.
[57] For example, see Barrington-Ward, *Love Will Out*, 184–96.

cannot bear the full weight of God's mission alone. Land speaks of the way in which local workings of the Spirit link with a much wider cosmic drama: 'Specific instances of the gifts of the Spirit operating in a worship setting or in the market place of witness, these particular instances are seen as part of a larger cosmic drama in which one is a participant and not a victim.'[58] Hence, we need to see a particular community's involvement in mission as it relates to a 'cosmic drama' that encompasses the mission of all Christ's people around the world. Just as in the local church it is the case that 'to each one of us grace has been given as Christ apportioned it' (Eph. 4:7) so in the global church gifts of evangelism, theology, wisdom, social insight and so on have been apportioned to different churches around the country and the world. This sharing comes under the biblical theme of *koinonia* (fellowship) that embraces the worldwide church and not just the local church. From this theme comes the need for partnership, for a working together, that Andrew Kirk argues is at the heart of what the church is.[59] For all Christians are called 'into the fellowship [*koinonia*] of his Son, Jesus Christ our Lord' (1 Cor. 1:9). The most basic meaning of *koinonia* is '"partaking together in" a group which has a common identity, goals and responsibilities'.[60] This picks up on the shared vision, values and functions already articulated. It is notable that *koinonia* involves both sharing the good blessings (cf. 1 Cor. 12:7) and the sufferings (2 Cor. 1:7; Col. 1:24; Phil. 3:10). We need churches that are both prepared to share the blessings they have received with, say, the people of Iraq and yet also share in the sufferings; to celebrate the blessings of growth of the church in southern Sudan and yet yearn that their suffering might end.

Much has been written of this partnership in blessings and sufferings and the principles of partnership identified by the Anglican Consultative Council can be seen to arise naturally out of the mission of the Spirit we have been developing:[61]

---

[58] Land, *Pentecostal Spirituality*, 137.

[59] Kirk, *Mission*, 186–7.

[60] Ibid., 188.

[61] A summary from the more detailed discussion in Johnson and Clark (eds.), *Anglicans in Mission*, 65.

(1)   The responsibility for mission in any place belongs
      primarily to the church in that place.
(2)   However, the universality of the gospel and the
      oneness of God's mission mean also that this mission
      must be shared in each and every place with fellow
      Christians from each and every part of the world with
      their distinctive insights and contributions.
(3)   We all have things to receive and things to give
      within the missionary task.

How this works in practice continues to be debated, but my primary argument here is that charismatic mission communities need
to be characterised by a desire for partnership that reflects the Spirit's
yearning for unity. This desire needs encouraging in both informal
and structural ways.[62] It is particularly required because of the overlaps that I assume will exist between charismatic mission
communities – for example, cell, Alpha and leadership communities may well also be part of a larger local church community.

Summary of Themes

I have been arguing that the mission of the Spirit naturally takes
place through communities.[63] Through a re-examination of the
voluntary principle in the light of pentecostal experience I have
suggested six Spirit-formed characteristics of charismatic mission
communities. These characteristics fit with the Spirit's yearning for
unity that means that communities will desire partnership with
other communities. This partnership may be informal but can be
seen as the basis for structures that enable both individual community life and expressions of the unity in the Spirit.[64] In the model

---

[62]   For some practical examples see Andrew M. Lord, *Spirit, Kingdom and
Mission: A Charismatic Missiology* (Cambridge: Grove, 2002), 18–21.
[63]   I have not addressed the related issue of election, the choice of a particular community for the sake of the world, and Newbigin provides much
insight here, *The Gospel in a Pluralist Society* (London: SPCK, 1989), 80ff.
[64]   Note that in Anglican terms I am suggesting a move from partnership
to structure rather than structure to partnership as has usually been the case
in the Partnership in Mission movement.

being developed here, both individual and partnered communities live within the mission of the Spirit that is forever reaching out into the world with Christ's love.

8

Mission Spirituality

A shop-keeper paid the church a compliment to Mary Mallon ...
'Oh!' said the shopkeeper, 'you can tell St Thomas's people quite easily
when they come in the shop.' Mary pressed for an explanation of how
this was possible. 'Well,' came the reply, 'they have a peace and a sense
of purpose in life that makes them different from others.' I am sure that
is not always true of all of us all the time; but I rejoice that it shows. It is
why we are in business.[1]

Mission becomes real in everyday Christian life. We need to find
ways of linking our vision and theology with what we might call the
'ordinary spirituality', life in the Spirit, of individuals and communities. Mission and spirituality are naturally connected by the work
of the Holy Spirit: our Christian mission and life are to be 'in the
Spirit' and integrated together. Mursell draws on the biblical testimony regarding the Holy Spirit in his approach to spirituality seen
as life in the Spirit that transforms us in the likeness of Christ in a
way that reflects God's glory to the world. The key to this life is
prayer and its fruit is holiness.[2] Without spirituality, mission can revert to activism that is somehow separate from everyday life, yet
without mission, spirituality can become a personal pursuit that has
no impact on the world. In this chapter I want to explore the two
themes of holiness and prayer with my model of mission as a way of
bringing mission and spirituality closer together.

There are many understandings of the term 'spirituality' and its
meaning has changed over time. For our purposes the definition of

---

[1] Robert Warren, *In the Crucible* (Crowborough: Highland, 1989), 135.
[2] Gordon Mursell, *English Spirituality: From Earliest Times to 1700* (London: SPCK, 2001), 9–11.

Gordon Wakefield may best help us forwards: 'spirituality concerns the way in which prayer influences conduct, our behaviour and manner of life, our attitudes to other people.'[3] This is a holistic definition of which only certain aspects tend to be appreciated by different pentecostal writers. In particular, there is a tendency to see spirituality in terms of either actions or affections. Russell Spittler argues that spirituality 'focuses on the pietistic habits of ordinary individuals'.[4] The habits or practices that he focuses on include speaking in tongues, baptism in the Holy Spirit, prayer for healing and words of knowledge. These are informed by five values that he sees as key to pentecostalism: experience, orality, spontaneity, otherworldliness and biblical authority. This approach helps us to see the practical nature of spirituality and the importance, in our context, of developing habits for mission. We have previously noted the approach of Land who focuses on inner 'distinctive apocalyptic affections' of gratitude, compassion and courage that are informed and shaped by pentecostal beliefs.[5] Land goes beyond the individual focus of Spittler to think about the characteristics of a missionary fellowship within which the affections are nurtured. Although he has less to say about practical actions, his summary theme is one of developing a 'passion for the kingdom' which fits well with the holistic action in mission explored earlier in this book.

There is much that could be explored along these lines but my aim here is to develop a few thoughts based around our framework for the mission of the Spirit which can also be seen as a framework for life in the Spirit. We can see charismatic spirituality in terms of two movements of the Spirit that are joined through a place of wait-ing on the Spirit. This can be represented graphically:

---

[3] Quoted in Cheslyn Jones, Geoffrey Wainwright and Edward Yarnold (eds.), *The Study of Spirituality* (London: SPCK, 1992), xxvi.

[4] R.P. Spittler, 'Spirituality, Pentecostal and Charismatic' in Burgess and van der Maas (eds.), *Dictionary of Pentecostal and Charismatic Movements*, 1096.

[5] Land, *Pentecostal Spirituality*, 23.

I want to explore some themes within a charismatic mission spirituality under the headings of attractive holiness, waiting on Pentecost and intercessory ministry. These three themes embrace respectively the aspects of worship, word and ministry that we saw as central to John Wimber's spirituality and liturgy. They are also suggestive of the traditional Three Ways in spirituality: the purgative, illuminative and unitive ways. Simon Chan links these to pentecostal spirituality through a consideration of 'baptism in the Spirit' and speaking in tongues. Whilst some of the links here may be tenuous there is enough to justify this approach to spirituality as being rooted in both pentecostal and wider traditions, if open to new insights. The overall sense in this spirituality is of a movement of the Spirit from God through the particular into all the world and back again to God. There are stopping points and no guarantee that all movement will be in the same direction, only the promise that God will be with us by the Spirit in all things.

Attractive Holiness

In Chapter 4 we explored the movement from the universal to the particular and suggested that holistic mission needed to embrace worship and love.[6] The mission of the Spirit challenges us to develop both affections and actions that speak of the attractiveness of God that will be fully seen in the kingdom to come. As the coming kingdom is one of light, love, worship and holiness it is not surprising that the mission of the *Holy* Spirit should also transform us in the process of reaching out to others. The pentecostal movement has had an emphasis both on mission and on holiness, perhaps in large part inherited from the Wesleyan Holiness revival movement of

---

[6] Points (6) and (7) in Chapter 4.2.

the nineteenth century. C.E. Jones suggests that this revival 'traced the church's malady to a lack of the marks of sanctification'.[7] Walter Hollenweger takes a wider understanding of the Holiness movement, taking it to embrace catholic, evangelical, critical and ecumenical strands.[8] But like others he points to the way in which the term 'baptism in the Spirit' developed from being a 'second religious crisis experience' for sanctification in the Holiness movement into one related to mission.[9] The link between holiness and mission seems a creative one that is worthy of further exploration. There is only space here to give some broad brush-strokes of how a spirituality of attractive holiness may be developed.

The term 'holiness' has a number of meanings and many aspects and here I want suggestively to link it with the nature and character of the coming kingdom outlined in Chapter 4. Here is a holiness that is personal, social and ecological, never separated from the holiness of God. This understanding of holiness goes beyond the typically individual approaches that many charismatics are familiar with and embraces the community and the earth. It is about the whole created order being transformed into the patterns of God, reflecting his purity, unity and grace. There is a holistic abundance of God's blessings which we yearn for and as we taste more of them so we are transformed in holiness. In terms of our spirituality the question is: what actions and affections can help us to grow in holiness in such a way that the mission of the Spirit is enabled? Here I want to point to two: the Eucharist as a place of thanksgiving and blessing; and the community as a place of holy relationships.

The Eucharist has not been explored in great depth in pentecostal and charismatic literature.[10] It is interesting to note that the article on the sacraments in the *Dictionary of Pentecostal and Charismatic*

---

[7] C.E. Jones, 'Holiness Movement' in Burgess and van der Maas (eds.), *Dictionary of Pentecostal and Charismatic Movements*, 726.

[8] Hollenweger, *Pentecostalism*, 2.

[9] Ibid., 182. For more detail on this see Faupel, *Everlasting Gospel*, 44–76.

[10] A notable exception is Christopher Cocksworth, *Evangelical Eucharistic Thought in the Church of England* (Cambridge: Cambridge University Press, 1993), whose study focuses on Anglican evangelical/charismatic developments. Steven takes a more charismatic focus, again Anglican, but his study is notable for its lack of Eucharistic thought: Steven, *Worship in the Spirit*.

Movements outlines the Roman Catholic viewpoint since 'there are no common [pentecostal] answers to questions concerning the nature, number, or efficacy of the sacraments'.[11] Another article suggests that pentecostals have been preoccupied with questions of whether the bread should be unleavened and the wine fermented, rather than any deeper theological reflection.[12] Chan moves thinking forward in challenging pentecostals to 'appropriate the experiential reality from eucharistic observances' and here I want to explore the link between the Eucharist and the blessings brought by the Spirit.[13] In this regard, David Ford provides a good starting point when he states that:

> Perhaps the best summary of what happens in the eucharist is: *The blessing of Jesus Christ* ... God blesses and is blessed, we bless and are blessed, creation blesses and is blessed, and a glorious ecology of blessing is the climactic vision of the Kingdom of God ... The eucharist generates a habitus of blessing and offers a hospitality which incorporates people and the material world by blessing.[14]

In the action of the Eucharist we open ourselves to the blessings of Jesus by the Holy Spirit. As we live again through the story of Jesus' life, death and resurrection so by the Spirit can our story be filled with the yearnings and blessings of God. The natural charismatic hesitancy about liturgy might begin to object that the Spirit is restricted with the repetition of the same words at each Eucharist. Whilst admitting the need for space for 'charismatic responses' to be built into the liturgy it is important to note what Ford says about 'non-identical repetition'.[15] The blessings of God are so great that each time we repeat the Eucharist a different aspect of these blessings can be received: the Eucharist is '"overdetermined" in its significance'.[16]

---

[11] F.A. Sullivan, 'Sacraments' in Burgess and van der Maas (eds.), *Dictionary of Pentecostal and Charismatic Movements*, 1033.

[12] P.D. Hocken, 'Ordinances, Pentecostal' in ibid., 948.

[13] Chan, *Pentecostal Theology*, 96.

[14] David F. Ford, *Self and Salvation: Being Transformed* (Cambridge: Cambridge University Press, 1999), 156.

[15] Ibid., 152–7.

[16] Ibid., 145.

What the Eucharist can help us to see and live out is that the blessings are always shaped around the life, death and resurrection of Jesus Christ. These blessings came and come into particular focus at the Last Supper but are to spread out through our lives into the world. We are to pattern our lives within the mission of the Spirit so that the blessings of God transform us in holiness and bring holiness to the world. Ford develops an approach to the Eucharist that leads to a 'transformed self', a self that 'is blessed and blesses'.[17] Such a 'eucharistic self', I suggest, is at the heart of what it means to be caught up in the mission of the Spirit in the ways we have been exploring through this book. The challenge is to become people of blessing and thanksgiving, immersed in the abundance of God and so transformed in holiness to do his will in the world. Such people cannot but attract others to Jesus Christ.

Ford usefully focuses on individual transformation in holiness in a way that links with the theme of blessing that has been explored through this book. Yet we also need transformed communities of holiness, as we discussed in the last chapter. Tim Dakin develops this idea in a general way as he argues that the fundamental condition on which the missionary enterprise depends is 'a mission spirituality embodied in a community of people committed to mission service'.[18] His approach builds on the call to transformed lives seen in Romans 12:2 and applies it to understanding church as a community in which the 'quest for truth [is] lived out in the drama of God's mission'.[19] This quest is shaped around 'the practical response to Jesus as Lord in a given context' lived out within the 'relational ethos' of church communities.[20] Dakin draws on 1 Peter to outline the ethos of a mission spirituality and he suggests that:

> I believe that we are now in the era of generating the ethos of holy community ... We find, scattered in chapters one and two of 1 Peter, five values of Christian community which characterise the ethos of the spiritual house of the living stones: word ('obeying the truth', 1:22),

---

[17] Ibid., 162.
[18] Tim Dakin, 'Encouraging Mission Mindedness: The Quest for an Ethos of Mission Spirituality in the Church', *CMS Newsletter* 554 (2003), 5 (CMS).
[19] Ibid., 13.
[20] Ibid., 12, 16.

'with-othering' ('genuine mutual love', 1:22), worship ('offering spiritual sacrifices', 2:5), witness ('proclaim the praises', 2:9) and work
('live such good lives', 2:11). This is the 'House of Holiness'.[21]

A spirituality that develops actions based on these values will be one
that roots itself deeper in the mission of the Spirit. This call to holiness can become the basis of evangelism, the call to join a people
caught up in the mission of the Spirit, transformed in holiness in response to Christ. Responding to Christ cannot be isolated from a
spirituality of holiness and the move of the Spirit into the world. A
mission spirituality demands that we develop hearts of openness and
thankfulness and ensure that our lives include patterns of holy listening, relating and Eucharist.

Waiting for Pentecost

Our life of mission in the Spirit should not be one of frantic activity,
as we are more concerned with the mission of the Spirit than what
our mission can achieve. The natural rush to do things needs to be
countered with a spirituality of waiting, a waiting for God's guiding
and empowering. The pattern for this is, of course, Pentecost, before which surprisingly the disciples were commanded to wait
before they rushed out in mission. This is a waiting in the hope of
blessings as the Spirit directs that picks up on the Old Testament
waiting based on the many promises of restoration. Wright sees this
theme of restoration as being key to understanding the ministry of
Jesus and the pentecostal scholar John Penney sees the theme of restoration introduced in Acts 2:1, which he translates, 'When the day
of Pentecost was being fulfilled.'[22] Penney argues for a link between
the Pentecost 'theophanic manifestations' and those seen at the
law-giving on Sinai. This also connects Pentecost with 'the Isaianic
promise that the law shall go forth from Jerusalem in the new age
from a restored Israel'.[23] He continues, 'The outpoured Spirit at

---

[21] Ibid., 19.
[22] N.T. Wright, *Jesus*, 125–31. Penney, *Missionary Emphasis*, 78. For further details of the debate here see Joseph A. Fitzmyer, *The Acts of the Apostles* (New York: Doubleday, 1998), 232–4.
[23] Cf. Isaiah 42:1–6; Penney, *Missionary Emphasis*, 80.

Pentecost is first of all the sign that Israel's mission to the nations has been re-inaugurated through the disciples of Jesus and the blessings of the new age have begun to flow.'[24] The long wait is over and the fulfilment of prophecy marks the start of a mission to the world that will draw people into the 'restored Israel'. The key to this mission is reception of the Holy Spirit, and 'the Holy Spirit is not simply the empowering of the messenger, but the power of the message for salvation, so that we may understand the Spirit also as the mediator of the promised Abrahamic blessings to the families of the earth'.[25] These blessings come first to those disciples gathered together obeying Jesus' command to wait, then spread from 'house to house' and 'in every city'[26] and indeed throughout the world as represented by the people gathered in Jerusalem at that time. The blessing was of a 'baptism in the Spirit' initially characterised by the disciples beginning 'to speak in other tongues as the Spirit enabled them' (2:4). This basic blessing was one that enabled the nations to hear 'the wonders of God,' to respond and become part of the people of God, the church. It is an eschatological blessing that had been long awaited, as seen in Peter's use of the quotation from Joel.[27] Waiting has led to the coming of blessings for the whole world through the eschatological Spirit.

Chan argues that the full benefit of Pentecost has not been reaped in pentecostal spirituality because of the focus of Spirit-baptism as being a one-off event in the early stages of spiritual life.[28] There is a need to find ways of building Spirit-baptism into the regular, on-going, life of individuals and churches. He argues for a sacramental understanding of Spirit-baptism that gets around some of the debate over the meaning of the term 'baptism in the Spirit'. The challenge is then to find ways of waiting and openness to this sacrament. Chan suggests a fuller appreciation is needed of the *epiclesis* in the Eucharist which may help develop themes from the last section. The invocation of the Holy Spirit on the people gathered, as well as the elements, is a part of some liturgies and this could be followed with a time of waiting. Yet maybe we also need to build

---

[24] Ibid., 95.
[25] Ibid.
[26] Acts 20:20, 8:40, 15:36.
[27] Fitzmyer, *Acts*, 252.
[28] Chan, *Pentecostal Theology*, 74.

into our lives specific times of waiting and seeking a fresh 'baptism' or filling with the Spirit. It is worth keeping the term baptism, even if it is as a metaphor for being soaked, covered and immersed in the Spirit. As we wait we can draw on the wisdom of contemplative spirituality, which one author has characterised as 'silent waiting' in the manner of the Psalmist.[29]

This waiting on God for the blessings brought by the Spirit may be characterised by yearnings as we are more aware of the needs than the fulfilment. The classic text that brings together personal and cosmic yearning in the hope of blessing is Romans 8:18–39. Gordon Fee suggests that the most traceable influence on Paul's understanding of the Spirit is the Old Testament presentation of 'the Spirit as the key to Israel's eschatological future'.[30] Qumran saw itself as fulfilling some of these prophecies, although as Terence Paige comments 'the difference for Paul is that the Spirit represents the inbreaking of the end time in the present'.[31] In Romans 8 Paul turns to a comparison between 'the sufferings of this present time' and 'the glory about to be revealed in us' (8:18). Having been speaking about individual struggle, Paul now puts this in the context of the whole of creation. The whole of creation is in 'bondage to decay' and is 'groaning in labour pains', just as we also groan in present sufferings (vv. 21–23). But there is *hope*, that creation will be set free and we will receive adoption and redemption of our bodies (vv. 21, 23). The present and the future are connected by hope, which implies the need for patient waiting in the present (v. 25). And yet Paul is telling believers that they are not left alone in the present, to sit around in suffering waiting for better things in the future. Paul has already spoken of the difference that the Spirit makes to Christian living (8:1–17) and now speaks of believers having the 'first fruits of the Spirit' (v. 23). Hope has a basis in the experience of the Spirit in the present – the 'first harvest in the present' that guarantees the 'fi-

---

[29] Alexander Ryrie, *Silent Waiting: The Biblical Roots of Contemplative Spirituality* (Norwich: Canterbury Press, 1999).

[30] Gordon D. Fee, *God's Empowering Presence* (Massachusetts: Hendrickson, 1994), 910.

[31] T. Paige, 'Holy Spirit' in Gerald F. Hawthorne, Ralph P. Martin and Daniel G. Reid (eds.), *Dictionary of Paul and his Letters* (Leicester: InterVarsity Press, 1993), 411.

nal eschatological harvest in the future'.[32] Paul's arguments about resurrection, adoption and redemption are here brought together in an eschatological tension between the present and the future: 'Already' we experience something of God's 'new epoch', although there is much that is 'not yet' seen. Charismatic mission spirituality involves being deeply led by the Spirit into the yearnings of the world, finding in Christ the hope for the future, and longing for a fresh immersion in the Spirit that blessings may be seen. This begins to address Chan's challenge that pentecostals need to take on board the 'dark night' in their spirituality.[33]

Intercessory Ministry

The Spirit's movement from the particular to the universal is grasped and appreciated through many different kinds of ministry. Whatever the ministry, it is important that they be grounded in prayer and are in some sense 'intercessory'. I want to start here with the gift of tongues that is an important part of charismatic spirituality and which Chan links with the unitive way, the move towards the integrated universal.[34] Tongues are often seen in personal terms, as a personal language of prayer and praise. This builds on Paul's argument in 1 Corinthians 14 where Fee suggests his argument is that tongues is primarily for the person speaking rather than for the wider Christian community.[35] However, some leeway is given by means of interpretation by which the community can be built up. Fee gives even greater scope to the practice of tongues in his interpretation of Romans 8:26, 'Likewise the Spirit helps us in our weakness; for we do not know how to pray as we ought, but that very Spirit intercedes with sighs too deep for words.' We have considered this section in terms of waiting, but there is also a sense of movement. Although the interpretation of this verse varies greatly it does seem fair to charismatic experience to allow for Fee's understanding here of tongues being a way in which the Spirit intercedes with sighs too deep for words.[36] This then links with the wider con-

---

[33] Chan, *Pentecostal Theology*, 75.
[34] Ibid., 76.
[35] Fee, *God's Empowering Presence*, 223.
[36] Ibid., 584–5.

text in which 'the whole creation has been groaning in labour pains' and in which 'we ourselves … groan inwardly' (Rom. 8:22–23). The particular experience of tongues in prayer and praise can be caught up in the yearnings and blessings of the Spirit in such a way as to move outwards and encompass all things in their pain and joy. Tongues need not be a mark of personal charismatic experience but can drive us out to embrace the world within the arms of God.

I want now to suggest, following Chan, although in a different way, that this practice of tongues can be enhanced through the practice and the understanding associated with the orthodox Jesus Prayer. Simply stated, this prayer involves saying the phrase 'Lord Jesus Christ, have mercy on me' repeatedly so that all this phrase represents becomes part of our heart-living and not just our mind.[37] Mark Cartledge notes how both the Jesus Prayer and the practice of tongues involve a repetition of words that enable a 'negation of the "self"' so that 'the person focuses on God rather than him or her-self'.[38] This prayer in orthodox tradition has often centred on particular individual transformation, although its link with the unity of creation points it outwards.[39] Simon Barrington-Ward, an Anglican missionary leader and later bishop, developed this outward aspect of the prayer subsequently to his charismatic experience alongside David Watson. For him all prayer is 'a sharing in a movement of love working through history'.[40] In a similar way to that which I suggested for tongues, Barrington-Ward speaks of how the Jesus Prayer 'moves in a twofold rhythm: thanksgiving and worship on the one hand – quiet, wordless love that has been called silent music, but bursts of joy and praise – and, on the other hand, a response of deep yearning and longing, and pain that so much of the world is absent from that light and joy'.[41] Here we have the blessings and yearnings that have helped shape the approach to mission in

---

[37] A fuller version of this prayer is 'Lord Jesus Christ, Son of God, have mercy on me, a sinner.' I prefer the shorter version with two equal phrases but there are other variations.

[38] Mark J. Cartledge, *Charismatic Glossolalia: An Empirical-Theological Study* (Aldershot: Ashgate, 2002), 188.

[39] Kallistos Ware, *The Power of the Name* (Oxford: SLG Press, 1986), 12–16.

[40] Barrington-Ward, *Love Will Out*, 30.

[41] Ibid., 32.

this book seen and experienced in prayer as well as in the world. Somehow the 'macrocosm' of the world and the 'microcosm' of ourselves can come together and inform and transform each other in our lives of prayer. As they do so the blessings and yearnings of ourselves and the world are held together at the cross of Christ, the only place at which these can be held with justice being done to both. Only at the cross can the 'now' and 'not yet' of Romans 8 be held together with particular and universal significance.[42]

This approach to prayer is both powerful and all-encompassing, drawing our whole lives deeper into the life of God in the whole of this world. But it is not an approach that is for everyone and indeed it may not seem that accessible. A more obvious way of praying that moves us in the Spirit from the particular to the universal is the evangelical approach to intercessory prayer. David Gillett suggests that 'more than any other spiritual tradition evangelicalism has earned the right to be called a spirituality of intercession'.[43] It has the power to move people from 'the cult of narcissistic self-culture' to 'extending the boundaries of the kingdom of God into the world'.[44] It is also an approach that is importantly practised in group contexts, seen in the great importance placed on the 'prayer meeting'.[45] A spirituality that finds out about the world both in general terms (as in *Operation World*)[46] and through the support of particular mission partners and turns this into prayer practises a significant outward movement in line with the mission of the Spirit. Such intercessory prayer complements the more contemplative approach represented by the Jesus Prayer, and indeed Gillett suggests the need to bring both together.[47]

Given the presence of such prayer that moves us outwards in mission into the world, ministry is a response to the call of God discerned in prayer, a way of serving God and others that cannot rest

---

[42] For a good introduction to this approach to the Jesus Prayer see Simon Barrington-Ward, *The Jesus Prayer* (Oxford: Bible Reading Fellowship, 1996).

[43] David Gillett, *Trust and Obey* (London: Darton, Longman & Todd, 1993), 189.

[44] Ibid., 190.

[45] Ibid., 172.

[46] Patrick Johnson, *Operation World* (Carlisle: OM, 1995).

[47] Gillett, *Trust and Obey*, 193.

until God's blessings are shared by all and all are brought together under Christ's Lordship.[48] Ministry is not divided up into 'pastoral' and 'missionary' or 'lay' and 'clergy' but rather encompasses each of these under the banner of ever-expanding blessing. The distinguishing factor in ministry is the call and gifting of the Spirit who unites the ministry of the church whilst sending each out in different ways of service. Much has been written on the subject of ministry and my purpose here is not to explore this in detail, but rather simply to see how ministry can be seen in intercessory ways within the mission of the Spirit.

Summary of Themes

The mission of the Spirit involves us being transformed as people of the Spirit. As people transformed by the Spirit we cannot but be a part of the mission of the Spirit. Mission and spirituality are vitally linked in a way that is not usually explored in books on the theology of mission. In this chapter I have outlined how a theology of mission and spirituality can be linked through the exploration of a few themes. As we reflect on the God of blessing so may we become a people of attractive holiness; as we wait, yearning for more of God, so may we become a people of Pentecost; and as we open ourselves to the world, may we become a people of intercessory ministry, so that the whole earth may be filled with the glory of God.

---

[48] For further reflections on this outlook see Christopher Cocksworth and Rosalind Brown, *Being a Priest Today: Exploring Priestly Identity* (Norwich: Canterbury Press, 2002), Part I.

9

Mission of the Spirit

In this book I have been developing a holistic charismatic theology of mission that builds on the wider pentecostal desire for a more holistic approach to mission. The framework developed provides an approach to mission that is holistic in terms of its content, outworkings, agency and life. The content of mission includes evangelism, healing, and social, reconciling and ecological action. All these are worked out in relation to specific contexts and embrace both particular and universal settings. Mission is tasted in both transcendent and immanent experiences of God that move creation towards the coming kingdom. It is carried out by individuals and communities as they embrace a spirituality for mission that affects the whole of life. Although this book only begins to address these many issues, it shows how a holistic approach to mission can be held together within a consistent framework. The framework developed also relates to wider debates in the theology of mission and the desire has been to draw together some of the pentecostal and ecumenical insights into mission through a focus on the mission of the Spirit within a setting of the 'creative tension' that David Bosch saw as central to any contemporary theology of mission. Starting with the mission of the Spirit, seen in terms of movements between the particular and the universal, it is possible to catch a vision of mission that goes beyond some of the divides of the past. In concluding I want to draw together insights on the mission of the Spirit glimpsed through this book and explore how they relate to some non-Western thinking.

Mission Vision

The framework for mission developed through this book is simply represented as follows:

Mission Movements of the Spirit

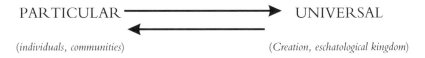

PARTICULAR ⟶ UNIVERSAL

(individuals, communities)   *(Creation, eschatological kingdom)*

The Holy Spirit is working to bring tastes of the holistic eschatological kingdom into the lives of individuals and communities today. The Spirit is also working within cultural contexts and particular experiences to move people out into the world and with the whole creation move towards the kingdom that is to come. The mission of God, *missio Dei*, is shaped primarily by the movements of the Spirit. The mission of Christians and the church is a participation in this mission as it inspires and challenges us to move on from where we are – in mission we are sent into these great movements of God. These movements are both 'life-giving' and also 'critical prophetic' as they encounter the present reality of the world. To use the metaphors I have been developing, the movements of the Spirit are characterised by tremendous blessings and yet also deep yearnings. These blessings are many faceted and can be summarised under the headings used in Chapter 4:

1. The blessing of relationships with Christ that make real the presence of God and drive us deeper into the Scriptures and indeed the whole history of people's experiences and thinking on Christ.
2. The blessing of healing in all its fullness.
3. The blessing of social 'shalom', of justice and peace.
4. The blessing of reconciliation, the overcoming of barriers, the drawing together in unity.
5. The blessing of a renewed creation and fresh creativity in arts, music, etc.
6. The blessing of a heart full of praise and thankfulness.

7.   The blessing of transformed characters, of lives turned around to seek the good.

These blessings all come in power, in love, in mercy, in revelation, in renewal, and in many other ways. We cannot encompass the abundance of God but are constantly surprised by aspects of his provision and promise that we had not seen before. Yet this great vision is rooted in the reality of lives that yearn for it to be so when it remains not so. There are at least five aspects of this yearning within which our yearning and that of the Spirit can become one in mission:

1.   The yearning through suffering, expressed in many ways: sorrow, weariness, groaning, brokenness, hurt, hopelessness, injustice, war; yearning of individuals, communities and whole nations.

2.   The yearning due to specific sin, perhaps a sense of lostness before God; a yearning for forgiveness and a fresh start.

3.   The yearning due to the state of the church, which has lost its way, become out of touch with people or God.

4.   The yearning due to opposition, when the 'Powers' seem set against us, when Satan and the multidimensionality of the demonic seem most real.

5.   The yearning that goes alongside waiting for God, a yearning we are called to and yet struggle with.

The character of the mission of the Spirit is one of both holistic blessing and yearning, one that is sometimes experienced in challenging, prophetic, judging, liberating, critical ways and at other times in more life-giving, comforting, healing and growing ways. The latter highlights the fact that mission is not just about great highs (of blessing) or great lows (of yearning) but also about the 'ordinary' of human life in which the Spirit is at work in different ways.

Participation in the mission of the Spirit will be unique for each individual and community as they respond to God and their situation. The mission of the Spirit may begin through an individual or community's particular culture, or general experience, or religious experience (explicitly or implicitly) or ritual (e.g. the Eucharist). From there the Spirit takes people with blessing and yearning out into the whole of creation. This may be a physical move, a change of attitude, a new way of relating to the people around, involvement in social groups – missionary stories testify to a whole wealth of possibilities. It is a move that aims to direct the creation towards the 'new creation', the coming eschatological kingdom to which all blessings point. Yet mission isn't all about giving from a safe position of faith with no loose ends! The mission of the Spirit brings the experience of the world, indeed the whole creation, to bear on individuals, communities and churches. We wrestle with the questions that confront us because of people's yearnings – there is no safe place from the Spirit's challenge. At the same time, we glimpse in mission a hopeful future as the Spirit makes real the coming kingdom in everyday lives with blessings which are more than we can imagine.

Non-Western Theology

Walter Hollenweger sees the *promise* of pentecostal mission in its reliance on the Holy Spirit to provide all the church needs for its life and mission, but the main *problem* is its reluctance to allow authentic indigenous non-Western churches and theology to develop.[1] Any theology of mission in the contemporary world needs to embrace non-Western concerns and insights, a point that has been noted at different times through this book. Lamin Sanneh argues that the significance of the current worldwide expansion of Christianity can be seen through the indigenous discovery of Christianity.[2] It has been since colonialism ended and with the delayed effect of Bible translation in which indigenous names for God were used that Christianity has expanded so greatly in Africa.[3] Sanneh's argument means that we need to be cautious about globalising tendencies that suggest one form of Christian faith and mission can be generically applied across all cultures. Rather, we should recognise that there are diverse appropriations of the Christian faith within the global

---

[1] Hollenweger, *Pentecostalism*, 298–9.
[2] Lamin Sanneh, *Whose Religion is Christianity? The Gospel Beyond the West* (Grand Rapids: Eerdmans, 2003), 10.
[3] Ibid., 18.

expansion of Christianity. Seeking unity within this setting is not to champion one theology over another, but to develop inter-cultural theology within which one enters into another's theology to appreciate and allow it to help shape our own.[4] Such inter-cultural theology should, I suggest, enter into biblical theology and the traditions of Christian theology if it is to be authentically Christian. Through this book I have sought to bring my own theology into conversation with some wider charismatic, pentecostal, biblical and ecumenical theologies. Yet much more is needed in order to develop conversations with non-Western sources so as to shape charismatic and wider pentecostal theologies of mission in the world today.

Kirsteen Kim illustrates a way forward through her Western immersion in theologians of the Spirit in India.[5] Her seeking to bring three such theologians into conversation leads to insights on the mission of the Spirit in that context that may be usefully compared with the approach taken here. Kim studied the understandings of the Holy Spirit in the theologies of Stanley Samartha, Vandana and Samuel Rayan. The significant overlap between their theologies and mine is in their appreciation of the work of the Holy Spirit outside the church: 'In the Indian context the existence and universality of the Spirit is a given.'[6] This working of the Spirit in all things points to a holistic understanding of mission, particularly one that embraces dialogue, inculturation and liberation.[7] Kim suggests that the 'Indian contribution to mission pneumatology has been above all to connect mission and spirituality,'[8] a connection I have also sought to make explicit. Despite these overlaps there appears a difference of starting point in our theologies of mission. Kim's study illustrates a focus on the present experiential working of the Spirit in particular contexts. She concludes that:

> This study suggests a theology of mission that recognises its starting point can be none other than a particular experience of the Spirit in the

---

[4] Hollenweger, *Pentecostalism*, 81–3.

[5] Kirsteen Kim, *Mission in the Spirit: The Holy Spirit in Indian Christian Theologies* (Delhi: ISPCK, 2003).

[6] Ibid., 235.

[7] Ibid., 241.

[8] Ibid., 242.

world, and that interacts with other such contextual theologies. These are not primarily biblical and historical but are contemporary theologies, arising in different geographical locations, social conditions and religious milieu, where the Spirit is at work.[9]

In contrast, I started with a biblical eschatological theology as a backdrop for considering particular experiences. Both approaches can be encompassed within the framework developed in this book, but the advantage of starting with a biblical eschatological vision is that it both supports Sanneh's argument regarding the centrality of the Bible in Christian expansion, and it gives a basis for discernment that both Kim and I see as of crucial importance in any theology of mission based on pneumatology. Within the joint emphasis on contextualisation, Kim's study suggests that my focus on the religious context of other faiths needs to be extended to a consideration of socio-political contexts. There is an 'inculturation–liberation' tension in mission that I have not had space to explore, but for which the three theologians Kim has studied have suggested 'pneumatological possibilities for transcending'.[10]

Alternative insights come from Allan Anderson's study of African Initiated Churches (AICs) which, while diverse in character, exhibit a 'biblical-African' alliance.[11] Anderson considers that 'AICs are mostly churches of a pentecostal type that have contextualized and indigenized Christianity.'[12] They stress a biblical basis, the 'freedom in the Spirit' and a 'spontaneously indigenous character' that resonate with the theology developed through this book. Anderson's conclusions fit in many ways with those of Sanneh on the growth of Christianity in places where traditional religious have significant influence, and also those of Harvey Cox, who links the growth of pentecostalism to its ability to relate to 'primal spirituality'.[13] The argument of the present book would be strengthened by linking my consideration of experience with others' considerations of primal/traditional religious experience. One aspect of AICs that

---

[9] Ibid., 242–3.
[10] Ibid., 237.
[11] Anderson, *African Reformation*, 194.
[12] Ibid., 207–8.
[13] Ibid., 209–10; Cox, *Fire from Heaven*, 81–2.

Inus Daneel considers its main theological contribution is the way they demonstrate 'how the gospel is adapted to or presented in confrontation with existing indigenous customs and values'.[14] Anderson outlines how this confrontational aspect is seen in relation to the practice of divination and ancestor observances. This confrontational aspect may cause us to review the arguments of Sanneh and Cox, although it does not negate the strongly indigenous character of AICs. In terms of the framework developed in this book, the confrontation represents the 'prophetic critical' working of the Spirit that has been developed. It also relates to the holistic opposition outlined in Chapter 4, in that AICs see certain tradition practices as 'expressions of real social malevolence and manifestations of evil spirits and sorcery'.[15] We examined the difference between confrontational and 'life-giving' approaches in Chapter 5, where I was wanting to correct the over-critical approach of some charismatics by a positive appreciation of Moltmann's ideas. But the 'prophetic critical' approach would benefit from further thought within my framework, perhaps linked with both an eschatological challenge and the victory of Christ achieved on the cross.

Final Thoughts

Douglas Jacobsen notes how 'Theology and experience deeply influenced each other within the pentecostal movement' and true to this insight this book started with my experience of mission and the search for theology alongside this.[16] In this book I have been developing a theology of mission that is rooted in experience but also challenges and develops the practice of mission. Although there are directions in which this theology needs to be stretched and deepened, the present framework embraces a holistic understanding of mission that can both affirm our present practices and draw us into new ways. For this to happen we need to be filled afresh with the Spirit of God. We need, as Simon Barrington-Ward has said, to be 'still and still moving'. To find a resting place in which we can be

---

[14] Quoted in Anderson, *African Reformation*, 195.

[15] Ibid., 194.

[16] Jacobsen, *Thinking in the Spirit*, 5.

shaped afresh by the mission of the Spirit and then hurled forward into things new; to adapt and discover fresh ways. The life of mission is an exciting and transforming one.

Come, Holy Spirit –
capture us afresh in your movements of mission.

Michael. Harpers book is dated 1968
Sale 1970s, & Rev 1980,
Most 1990s — 2005

What about 1906 — 1968 ?
Covering early Pentecostals
+ 2nd generation ones?

Bibliography

Allen, Roland, *Missionary Methods: St Paul's or Ours?* (Grand Rapids: Eerdmans, 1962)

Althouse, Peter, *Spirit of the Last Days* (London: T&T Clark, 2003)

Anderson, Allan, 'Global Pentecostalism in the New Millennium' in Allan H. Anderson and Walter J. Hollenweger (eds.), *Pentecostals After a Century: Global Perspectives on a Movement in Transition* (Sheffield: Sheffield Academic Press, 1999), 209–23

—, 'The Gospel and Culture in Pentecostal Mission in the Third World', *Missionalia* 27.2 (1999), 220–30

—, 'Signs and Blunders: Pentecostal Mission Issues at "Home and Abroad" in the Twentieth Century', *Journal of Asian Mission* 2.2 (2000), 193–210

—, *African Reformation: African Initiated Christianity in the 20th Century* (Asmara: Africa World Press, 2001)

—, *An Introduction to Pentecostalism* (Cambridge: Cambridge University Press, 2004)

Archbishops' Council, *Mission-Shaped Church: Church Planting and Fresh Expressions of Church in a Changing Context* (London: Church House, 2004)

Aune, David E., *Revelation 6–16* (Dallas: Word, 1998)

Bailyes, Alan J., 'Evangelical and Ecumenical Understandings of Mission', *International Review of Mission* 85.339 (1996), 485–503

Barrington-Ward, Simon, *Love Will Out* (Basingstoke: Marshall, Morgan & Scott, 1988)

—, *The Jesus Prayer* (Oxford: Bible Reading Fellowship, 1996)

Bauckham, Richard, 'Jürgen Moltmann' in David F. Ford (ed.), *The Modern Theologians* (Oxford: Blackwell, 1997), 209–24

—, 'Eschatology in *The Coming of God*' in Richard Bauckham (ed.), *God Will be All in All: The Eschatology of Jürgen Moltmann* (Edinburgh: T&T Clark, 1999), 1–34

—, 'Time and Eternity' in Richard Bauckham (ed.), *God Will be All in All: The Eschatology of Jürgen Moltmann* (Edinburgh: T&T Clark, 1999), 155–226

Beck, Brian E., '*Imitatio Christi* and the Lucan Passion Narrative' in William Horbury and Brian McNeil (eds.), *Suffering and Martyrdom in the New Testament* (Cambridge: Cambridge University Press, 1981), 28–47

Begbie, Jeremy S., *Theology, Music and Time* (Cambridge: Cambridge University Press, 2000)

Berkhof, Hendrikus, *The Doctrine of the Holy Spirit* (London: Epworth Press, 1965)

Bertone, John A., 'The Function of the Spirit in the Dialectic between God's Soteriological Plan Enacted but not yet Culminated: Romans 8:1–27'. *Journal of Pentecostal Theology* 15 (1999), 75–97

Bevans, Stephen B., *Models of Contextual Theology* (New York: Orbis, 1992)

Bock, D.L., 'Luke, Gospel of' in Green, Joel B., Scot McKnight and I. Howard Marshall (eds.), *Dictionary of Jesus and the Gospels* (Leicester: Inter-Varsity Press, 1992), 495–510

Bonino, José Míguez, 'Pentecostal Mission is More than what it Claims', *PNEUMA* 16.2 (1994), 283–8

Bosch, David, *Transforming Mission: Paradigm Shifts in Theology of Mission* (New York: Orbis, 1991)

Burgess, Stanley M. and Eduard M. van der Maas (eds.), *The New International Dictionary of Pentecostal and Charismatic Movements* (Grand Rapids: Zondervan, 2002)

Cartledge, Mark J., *Charismatic Glossolalia: An Empirical-Theological Study* (Aldershot: Ashgate, 2002)

—, *Practical Theology: Charismatic and Empirical Perspectives* (Carlisle: Paternoster Press, 2003)

Castro, Emilio, 'Editorial', *ER* 43.2 (April 1991), 163

Chan, Simon, 'An Asian Review [of *Spirit of Life*]', *Journal of Pentecostal Theology* 4 (1994), 35–40

—, *Pentecostal Theology and the Christian Spiritual Tradition* (Sheffield: Sheffield Academic Press, 2000)

Chester, Timothy, *Awakening to a World of Need: The Recovery of Evangelical Social Concern* (Leicester: Inter-Varsity Press, 1993)

Childs, Brevard S., *Isaiah* (Louisville: Westminster John Knox Press, 2001)

Cocksworth, Christopher, *Evangelical Eucharistic Thought in the Church of England* (Cambridge: Cambridge University Press, 1993)

—, *Holy, Holy, Holy: Worshipping the Trinitarian God* (London: Darton, Longman & Todd, 1997)

Cocksworth, Christopher and Rosalind Brown, *Being a Priest Today: Exploring Priestly Identity* (Norwich: Canterbury Press, 2002)

Coote, Robert T., 'Lausanne II and World Evangelization', *International Bulletin of Missionary Research* 14 (1990), 10–17

Corrie, John, 'Creative Tensions in the Mission of the Church: David Bosch Ten Years On', *ANVIL* 18.2 (2001), 97–106

Cottrell, Stephen, *Sacrament, Wholeness and Evangelism: A Catholic Approach* (Cambridge: Grove, 1996)

Cox, Harvey, *Fire from Heaven: The Rise of Pentecostal Spirituality and the Reshaping of Religion in the 21st Century* (London: Cassell, 1996)

—, 'Pentecostalism and Global Market Culture' in Dempster, Murray W., Byron D. Klaus and Douglas Petersen (eds.), *The Globilization of Pentecostalism: A Religion Made to Travel* (Oxford: Regnum, 1999), 386–96

Cray, Graham, *From Here to Where? The Culture of the Nineties* (London: Board of Mission, 1992)

—, 'New Churches for a New Millennium', *Anglicans for Renewal* 78 (1999), 15–18

Cross, Terry L., 'The Rich Feast of Theology: Can Pentecostals Bring the Main Course or Only the Relish?', *Journal of Pentecostal Theology* 16 (2000), 27–47

Cullmann, Oscar, 'Mission in God's Eschatology' in Norman Thomas (ed.), *Readings in World Mission* (London: SPCK, 1995), 307–9

Dakin, Tim, 'Mission Out of Order,' *CMS Newsletter* 551 (2001), 2–12

—, 'Communion in Mission,' *CMS Newsletter* 553 (2002), 2–23

—, 'Encouraging Mission Mindedness: The Quest for an Ethos of Mission Spirituality in the Church', *CMS Newsletter* 554 (2003), 2–24 (CMS)

Davis, J.R., *Poles Apart* (Bangalore: ATA, 1993)

Dayton, Donald W., *Theological Roots of Pentecostalism* (London: Scarecrow Press, 1987)

Dempster, Murray W., Byron D. Klaus and Douglas Petersen (eds.) *The Globalization of Pentecostalism: A Religion Made to Travel* (Oxford: Regnum, 1999)

Dempster, Murray W., Byron D Klaus and Douglas Petersen (eds.), *Called and Empowered: Global Mission in Pentecostal Perspective* (Sheffield: Sheffield Academic Press, 1991)

Dempster, Murray W., 'Evangelism, Social Concern and the Kingdom of God' in Dempster, Murray W., Byron D. Klaus and Douglas

Petersen (eds.), *Called and Empowered: Global Mission in Pentecostal Perspective* (Sheffield: Sheffield Academic Press, 1991), 22–43

Dillistone, F.W., *Into All the World: A Biography of Max Warren* (London: Hodder & Stoughton, 1980)

Douglas, J.D. (ed.), *Proclaim Christ until He Comes* (Minneapolis: World Wide, 1989)

Faupel, D. William, *The Everlasting Gospel: The Significance of Eschatology in the Development of Pentecostal Thought* (Sheffield: Sheffield Academic Press, 1996)

Fee, Gordon D., *God's Empowering Presence* (Massachusetts: Hendrickson, 1994)

Fitzmyer, Joseph A., *The Acts of the Apostles* (New York: Doubleday, 1998)

Ford, David F., *Self and Salvation: Being Transformed* (Cambridge: Cambridge University Press, 1999)

Freytag, Walter, 'Mission in View of the End' in Thomas, Norman (ed.), *Readings in World Mission* (London: SPCK, 1995), 309–11

Fulljames, Peter, *God and Creation in Intercultural Perspective* (Frankfurt: Peter Lang, 1993)

Gerloff, Roswith, 'Pentecostals in the African Diaspora' in Allan H. Anderson and Walter J. Hollenweger (eds.), *Pentecostals After a Century: Global Perspectives on a Movement in Transition* (Sheffield: Sheffield Academic Press, 1999), MS.40–61

Gibbs, Eddie, 'The Evangelist' in David Pytches (ed.), *John Wimber: His Influence and Legacy* (Guildford: Eagle, 1998), 71–83

Giddens, Anthony, *Sociology* (Cambridge: Polity Press, 1993)

Gillett, David, *Trust and Obey* (London: Darton, Longman & Todd, 1993)

Goff Jr., James R., *Fields White Unto Harvest: Charles F. Parham and the Missionary Origins of Pentecostalism* (Fayetteville: University of Arkansas Press, 1988)

Gumbel, Nicky, *The Heart of Revival* (Eastbourne: Kingsway, 1997)

Gunstone, John, *A People for His Praise: Renewal and Congregational Life* (London: Hodder & Stoughton, 1978)

—, *Signs and Wonders: The Wimber Phenomenon* (London: Daybreak, 1989)

Hagner, Donald A., *Matthew 1–13* (Dallas: Word, 1998)

Harper, Michael, *Walk in the Spirit* (London: Hodder & Stoughton, 1968)

—, *This is the Day: A Fresh Look at Christian Unity* (London: Hodder & Stoughton, 1979)

Head, Peter M., *Christology and the Synoptic Problem: An Argument for Markan Priority* (Cambridge: Cambridge University Press, 1997)

Hocken, P.D., *Streams of Renewal: The Origins and Early Development of the Charismatic Movement in Great Britain* (Carlisle: Paternoster Press, 1997)

—, 'Charismatic Movement' in Stanley M. Burgess and Eduard M. van der Maas (eds.), *The New International Dictionary of Pentecostal and Charismatic Movements* (Grand Rapids: Zondervan, 2002), 477–519

—, 'Church, Theology of the' in Stanley M. Burgess and Eduard M. van der Maas (eds.), *The New International Dictionary of Pentecostal and Charismatic Movements* (Grand Rapids: Zondervan, 2002), 544–51

—, 'Ordinances, Pentecostal' in Stanley M. Burgess and Eduard M. van der Maas (eds.), *The New International Dictionary of Pentecostal and Charismatic Movements* (Grand Rapids: Zondervan, 2002), 947–9

Hodges, Melvin L., *The Indigenous Church* (Springfield: Gospel, 1976)

Hollenweger, W.J., *Pentecostalism: Origins and Developments Worldwide* (Massachusetts: Hendrickson, 1997)

Hunter, Harold D. and Peter D. Hocken (eds.), *All Together in One Place: Theological Papers from the Brighton Conference on World Evangelization* (Sheffield: Sheffield Academic Press, 1993)

Inge, John, *A Christian Theology of Place* (Aldershot: Ashgate, 2003)

Jacobsen, Douglas, *Thinking in the Spirit: Theologies of the Early Pentecostal Movement* (Bloomington: Indiana University Press, 2003)

Johnson, Eleanor and John Clark (eds.), *Anglicans in Mission: A Transforming Journey; Report of MISSIO 1999* (London: SPCK, 2000)

Johnson, Patrick, *Operation World* (Carlisle: OM, 1995)

Johnson, Todd M., 'Global Plans in the Pentecostal/Charismatic Tradition and the Challenge of the Unevangelized World' in Jan A.B. Jongeneel (ed.), *Pentecost, Mission and Ecumenism*, (Frankfurt: Peter Lang, 1992)

Jones, C.E., 'Holiness Movement' in Stanley M. Burgess and Eduard M. van der Maas (eds.), *The New International Dictionary of Pentecostal and Charismatic Movements* (Grand Rapids: Zondervan, 2002), 726–9

Jones, Cheslyn, Geoffrey Wainwright and Edward Yarnold (eds.), *The Study of Spirituality* (London: SPCK, 1992)

Kärkkäinen, Veli-Matti, '"Truth on Fire": Pentecostal Theology of Mission and the Challenges of a New Millennium', *Asian Journal of Pentecostal Studies* 3.1 (2000), 33–60

—, 'Missiology: Pentecostal and Charismatic' in Stanley M. Burgess and Eduard M. van der Maas (eds.), *The New International Dictionary of Pentecostal and Charismatic Movements* (Grand Rapids: Zondervan, 2002), 877–85

—, *Pneumatology: The Holy Spirit in Ecumenical, International, and Contextual Perspective* (Grand Rapids: Baker, 2002)

Kim, Kirsteen, 'Post-Modern Mission: A Paradigm Shift in David Bosch's Theology of Mission' in Timothy Yates (ed.), *Mission – An Invitation to God's Future* (Sheffield: Cliff College, 2000), 99–108

—, *Mission in the Spirit: The Holy Spirit in Indian Christian Theologies* (Delhi: ISPCK, 2003)

Kirk, Andrew J., *What is Mission? Theological Explorations* (London: Darton, Longman & Todd, 1999)

Kraft, Charles, *Christianity with Power: Experiencing the Supernatural* (London: Marshall Pickering, 1990)

Kuzmic, Peter, 'A Croatian-War-Time Reading [of *Spirit of Life*]', *Journal of Pentecostal Theology* 4 (1994), 17–24

Ladd, George, *A Theology of the New Testament* (Guildford: Lutterworth Press, 1974)

Land, Steven J., *Pentecostal Spirituality: A Passion for the Kingdom* (Sheffield: Sheffield Academic Press, 1993)

Lapoorta, Japie J., 'An African Perspective [on *Spirit of Life*]', *Journal of Pentecostal Theology* 4 (1994), 51–8

Lawrence, Peter H., *Doing What Comes Supernaturally* (Bristol: Terra Nova, 1997)

Lincoln, Andrew T., *Ephesians* (Dallas: Word, 1998)

Lord, Andrew M., 'Mission Eschatology: A Framework for Mission in the Spirit', *Journal of Pentecostal Theology* 11 (1997), 111–23

—, 'Contextualisation in Britain: Insights from a Celtic Spirituality', MA dissertation (Birmingham, 1999)

—, 'Mission, the Bible and Israel-Palestine', *Evangelical Review of Theology* 24.2 (2000), 149–58

—, 'The Voluntary Principle in Pentecostal Missiology', *Journal of Pentecostal Theology* 17 (2000), 81–95

—, 'The Holy Spirit and Contextualisation', *Asian Journal of Pentecostal Studies* 4.2 (2001), 201–13

—, *Spirit, Kingdom and Mission: A Charismatic Missiology* (Cambridge: Grove, 2002)

—, 'Virtual Communities and Mission', *Evangelical Review of Theology* 26.3 (2002), 196–207

—, 'A Charismatic Approach to Other Faiths', *Asian Journal of Pentecostal Studies* 6.2 (2003)

—, 'The Moltmann-Pentecostal Dialogue: Implications for Mission', *Journal of Pentecostal Theology* 11.2 (2003), 271–87

Macchia, Frank D., 'A North American Response [to *Spirit of Life*]', *Journal of Pentecostal Theology* 4 (1994), 25–33

—, 'The Spirit and Life: A Further Response to Jürgen Moltmann', *Journal of Pentecostal Theology* 5 (1994), 121–7

—, 'The Struggle for Global Witness: Shifting Paradigms in Pentecostal Theology' in Murray W. Dempster, Byron D. Klaus and Douglas Petersen (eds.), *The Globilization of Pentecostalism: A Religion Made to Travel* (Oxford: Regnum, 1999), 8–29

Martin, David, *Pentecostalism: The World their Parish* (Oxford: Blackwell, 2002)

McClung Jr, L. Grant, 'Missiology' in S.M. Burgess, G.B. McGee and P.H. Alexander (eds.), *Dictionary of Pentecostal and Charismatic Movements* (Grand Rapids: Regency Reference Library, 1988), 607–9

—, 'Pentecostal/Charismatic Perspectives on a Missiology for the Twenty-First Century', *PNEUMA* 16 (Spring 1994), 11–21

—, '"Try to Get People Saved": Revisiting the Paradigm of an Urgent Pentecostal Missiology' in Murray W. Dempster, Byron D. Klaus and Douglas Petersen (eds.), *The Globilization of Pentecostalism: A Religion Made to Travel* (Oxford: Regnum, 1999), 30–51

McConnell, C. Douglas (ed.), *The Holy Spirit and Mission Dynamics* (Pasadena: William Carey Library, 1997)

McCoy, Michael, '"Community": A Postmodern Mission Paradigm?', *Journal of Anglican Studies* 1.1 (2003), 31–45

McGee, Gary B., 'Missions, Overseas (North American)' in S.M. Burgess, G.B. McGee and P.H. Alexander (eds.), *Dictionary of Pentecostal and Charismatic Movements* (Grand Rapids: Regency Reference Library, 1988), 610–25

—, 'Pentecostal Missiology: Moving Beyond Triumphalism to Face the Issues', *PNEUMA* 16.2 (1994), 275–81

—, '"Power from on High": A Historical Perspective on the Radical Strategy in Missions' in Wonsuk Ma and Robert P. Menzies (eds.), *Pentecostalism in Context: Essays in Honor of William W. Menzies* (Sheffield: Sheffield Academic Press, 1997), 317–36

McGrath, Alister, *Christian Theology: An Introduction* (Oxford: Blackwell, 1997²)

McIntyre, John, *The Shape of Pneumatology* (Edinburgh: T&T Clark, 1997)

Moltmann, Jürgen, *The Way of Jesus Christ* (London: SCM, 1990)

—, *The Spirit of Life: A Universal Affirmation* (London: SCM, 1992)

—, 'A Response to my Pentecostal Dialogue Partners', *Journal of Pentecostal Theology* 4 (1994), 59–70

—, 'A Pentecostal Theology of Life', *Journal of Pentecostal Theology* 9 (1996), 10–11

—, *The Coming of God: Christian Eschatology* (London: SCM, 1996)

—, 'The Bible, the Exegete and the Theologian' in Richard Bauckham (ed.), *God Will be All in All: The Eschatology of Jürgen Moltmann* (Edinburgh: T&T Clark, 1999), 227–32

—, 'The Mission of the Spirit: The Gospel of Life' in Timothy Yates (ed.), *Mission – An Invitation to God's Future* (Sheffield: Cliff College, 2000), 19–34

Moule, C.F.D., *The Holy Spirit* (London: Mowbrays, 1978)

Mursell, Gordon, *English Spirituality: From Earliest Times to 1700* (London: SPCK, 2001)

Naish, Tim, 'Ways Forward in Mission Studies: Theory or Image?', *Missiology* 27.2 (1999), 163–78

Neely, Alan and James A. Scherer, 'San Antonio and Manila 1989: " ... Like Ships in the Night?"', *Missiology* 18.2 (1990), 139–48

Newbigin, Lesslie, *The Gospel in a Pluralist Society* (London: SPCK, 1989)

Nichols, Alan (ed.), *The Whole Gospel for the Whole World: Story of Lausanne II Congress on World Evangelization* (Ventura: LCWE & Regal, 1989)

O'Brien, Peter T., *Colossians, Philemon* (Dallas: Word, 1998)

O'Collins, Gerald G., 'Salvation' in D.N. Freedman (ed.), *Anchor Bible Dictionary* (New York: Doubleday, 1992), 907–14

Paige, T., 'Holy Spirit' in Gerald F. Hawthorne, Ralph P. Martin and Daniel G. Reid (eds.), *Dictionary of Paul and his Letters* (Leicester: Inter-Varsity Press, 1993), 404–13

Parshall, Phil, *New Paths in Muslim Evangelism: Evangelical Approaches to Contextualization* (Grand Rapids: Baker, 1980)

Penney, John Michael, *The Missionary Emphasis of Lukan Pneumatology* (Sheffield: Sheffield Academic Press, 1997)

Petersen, Douglas, 'The Kingdom of God and the Hermeneutical Circle: Pentecostal Praxis in the Third World' in Murray W. Dempster, Byron D. Klaus and Douglas Petersen (eds.), *Called and Empowered: Global Mission in Pentecostal Perspective* (Sheffield: Sheffield Academic Press, 1991), 44–58

—, *Not by Might Nor by Power: A Pentecostal Theology of Social Concern in Latin America* (Oxford: Regnum, 1996)

—, 'Missions in the Twenty-First Century: Toward a Methodology of Pentecostal Compassion', *Transformation* 16.2 (1999), 54–9

Pinnock, Clark H., *Flame of Love: A Theology of the Holy Spirit* (Downers Grove: InterVarsity Press, 1996)

Plus, Jean-Daniel, 'Globalization of Pentecostalism or Globalization of Individualism? A European Perspective' in Murray W. Dempster, Byron D. Klaus and Douglas Petersen (eds.), *The Globlization of*

Pentecostalism: A Religion Made to Travel (Oxford: Regnum, 1999), 170–82

Pomerville, Paul A., *The Third Force in Missions* (Massachusetts: Hendrickson, 1985)

Porter, Matthew, *David Watson: Evangelism, Renewal, Reconciliation* (Cambridge: Grove, 2003)

Prior, Michael, *Jesus the Liberator: Nazareth Liberation Theology* (Sheffield: Sheffield Academic Press, 1995)

Pytches, David, *Come, Holy Spirit* (London: Hodder & Stoughton, 1995)

—, (ed.), *John Wimber: His Influence and Legacy* (Guildford: Eagle, 1998)

Riches, John, *Matthew* (Sheffield: Sheffield Academic Press, 1996)

Robeck, Cecil M., 'Pentecostal Origins from a Global Perspective' in Harold D. Hunter and Peter D. Hocken (eds.), *All Together in One Place: Theological Papers from the Brighton Conference on World Evangelization* (Sheffield: Sheffield Academic Press, 1993), 166–80

Ryrie, Alexander, *Silent Waiting: The Biblical Roots of Contemplative Spirituality* (Norwich: Canterbury Press, 1999)

Sanneh, Lamin, *Translating the Message* (New York: Orbis, 1989)

—, *Whose Religion is Christianity? The Gospel Beyond the West* (Grand Rapids: Eerdmans, 2003)

Saunders, Teddy and Hugh Sansom, *David Watson: A Biography* (London: Hodder & Stoughton, 1992)

Schreiter, Robert J., *Constructing Local Theologies* (New York: Orbis, 1985)

Schweizer, Eduard, 'On Distinguishing between Spirits', *Ecumenical Review* 41.3 (July 1989)

Sepúlveda, Juan, 'The Perspective of Chilean Pentecostalism [on *Spirit of Life*]', *Journal of Pentecostal Theology* 4 (1994), 41–9

Shorter, Aylward, *Toward a Theology of Inculturation* (New York: Orbis, 1988)

Sider, Ronald, *Evangelism and Social Action* (London: Hodder & Stoughton, 1993)

Simpson, Ray, *Exploring Celtic Spirituality: Historic Roots for Our Future* (London: Hodder & Stoughton, 1995)

Smail, Tom, 'The Devil you Think you Know: Demonology and the Charismatic Movement' in Tom Smail, Andrew Walker and Nigel Wright, *Charismatic Renewal: The Search for a Theology* (London: SPCK, 1993), 86–105

Spittler, R.P., 'Spirituality, Pentecostal and Charismatic' in Stanley M. Burgess and Eduard M. van der Maas (eds.), *The New International Dictionary of Pentecostal and Charismatic Movements* (Grand Rapids: Zondervan, 2002), 1096–102

Stanley, Brian, *The Bible and the Flag: Protestant Missions and British Imperialism in the Nineteenth and Twentieth Centuries* (Leicester: Inter-Varsity Press, 1990)

Stanton, Graham N., *A Gospel for a New People: Studies in Matthew* (Edinburgh: T&T Clark, 1992)

—, *The Gospels and Jesus* (Oxford: Oxford University Press, 2002)

Steven, James H.S., *Worship in the Spirit: Charismatic Worship in the Church of England* (Carlisle: Paternoster Press, 2002)

Stibbe, Mark, 'A British Appraisal [of *Spirit of Life*]', *Journal of Pentecostal Theology* 4 (1994), 5–16

—, *Revival* (Crowborough: Monarch, 1998)

Stott, John, 'Twenty Years after Lausanne: Some Personal Reflections', *International Bulletin of Missionary Research* 19.2 (1995), 50–55

Sullivan, F.A., 'Sacraments' in Stanley M. Burgess and Eduard M. van der Maas (eds.), *The New International Dictionary of Pentecostal and Charismatic Movements* (Grand Rapids: Zondervan, 2002), 1033–6

Suurmond, Jean-Jacques, *Word and Spirit at Play: Towards a Charismatic Theology* (London: SCM Press, 1994)

Taylor, John V., *The Primal Vision* (London: SCM, 1963)

—, *The Go-Between God: The Holy Spirit and the Christian Mission* (London: SCM, 1972)

Thomas, Norman E. (ed.), *Readings in World Mission* (London: SPCK, 1995)

—, 'World Mission Conferences: What Impact do they Have?', *International Bulletin of Missionary Research* 20 (1996), 146–54

Tomlinson, Anne L., *Training God's Spies: Developing the Imagination in Theological Formation* (Edinburgh: Contact Pastoral Trust, 2001)

Travis, S.H., *I Believe in the Second Coming of Jesus* (London: Hodder & Stoughton, 1982)

Turner, Max, *Power from on High: The Spirit in Israel's Restoration and Witness in Luke-Acts* (Sheffield: Sheffield Academic Press, 1996)

Urquhart, Colin, *When the Spirit Comes* (London: Hodder & Stoughton, 1974)

Utuk, Efiong S., 'From Wheaton to Lausanne: The Road to Modification of Contemporary Evangelical Mission Theology', *Missiology* 14.2 (1986), 205–20

Veenhof, Jan, 'The Significance of the Charismatic Renewal for Theology and Church' in Jan A.B. Jongeneel (ed.), *Pentecost, Mission and Ecumenism* (Frankfurt: Peter Lang, 1992)

Verseput, D., 'The Role and Meaning of the "Son of God" Title in Matthew's Gospel', *New Testament Studies* 33.4 (1987), 532–56

Wagner, C. Peter (ed.), *Spiritual Power and Church Growth* (London: Hodder & Stoughton, 1986)

—, *Territorial Spirits* (Chichester: Sovereign World, 1991)

Wakefield, Gavin, 'Mission in the Spirit: Revivalist and Celtic Strands of Mission', *ANVIL* 18.1 (2001), 7–20

Walls, Andrew F., *The Missionary Movement in Christian History* (Edinburgh: T&T Clark, 1996)

—, 'Converts or Proselytes? The Crisis over Conversion in the Early Church,' *IBMR* 28.1 (2004), 2–7

Ware, Kallistos, *The Power of the Name* (Oxford: SLG Press, 1986)

Warren, Max, *Crowded Canvas: Some Experiences of a Life-Time* (London: Hodder & Stoughton, 1974)

Warren, Robert, *In the Crucible* (Crowborough: Highland, 1989)

—, *Being Human, Being Church* (London: Marshall Pickering, 1995)

Watson, David, *I Believe in Evangelism* (London: Hodder & Stoughton, 1976)

—, *You are my God* (London: Hodder & Stoughton, 1983)

Westmeier, Karl-Wilhelm, 'Themes of Pentecostal Expansion in Latin America', *International Bulletin of Missionary Research* (April 1993), 72–8

Wilson, D.J., 'Eschatology, Pentecostal Perspectives on' in Stanley M. Burgess and Eduard M. van der Maas (eds.), *The New International Dictionary of Pentecostal and Charismatic Movements* (Grand Rapids: Zondervan, 2002), 601–5

Wimber, John and Kevin Springer, *Power Evangelism* (London: Hodder & Stoughton, 1985)

—, *Power Healing* (London: Hodder & Stoughton, 1986)

—, *The Dynamics of Spiritual Growth* (London: Hodder & Stoughton, 1990)

—, *Power Evangelism* (London: Hodder & Stoughton, 1992²)

Wingate, Andrew, *Encounter in the Spirit: Muslim–Christian Dialogue in Practice* (Geneva: WCC, 1988)

Wink, Walter, *Naming the Powers: The Language of Power in the New Testament* (Philadelphia: Fortress Press, 1984)

Wright, Nigel, 'The Theology and Methodology of "Signs and Wonders"' in Tom Smail, Andrew Walker and Nigel Wright, *Charismatic Renewal: The Search for a Theology* (London: SPCK, 1993), 71–85

Wright, N.T., *Colossians and Philemon* (Leicester: Inter-Varsity Press, 1986)

—, *The New Testament and the People of God* (London: SPCK, 1992)

—, *Jesus and the Victory of God* (London: SPCK, 1996)

—, *New Heavens, New Earth: The Biblical Picture of Christian Hope* (Cambridge: Grove, 1999)

—, *The Resurrection of the Son of God* (London: SPCK, 2003)

Yates, Timothy, *Christian Mission in the Twentieth Century* (Cambridge: Cambridge University Press, 1994)

Yong, Amos, *Discerning the Spirit(s), A Pentecostal-Charismatic Contribution to Christian Theology of Religions* (Sheffield: Sheffield Academic Press, 2000)

—, *Beyond the Impasse: Toward a Pneumatological Theology of Religion* (Carlisle: Paternoster, 2003)

Also in the *Studies in Pentecostal and Charismatic Issues* series

Practical Theology

Charismatic and Empirical Perspectives

Mark Cartledge

ISBN: 1-84227-200-4

This groundbreaking work is the first book on practical theology from a charismatic viewpoint. It is unique in integrating charismatic and empirical perspectives in practical theology, exemplifying both qualitative and quantitative methods of research. In Part One Mark Cartledge offers a proposal for practical theology, reviewing the ways in which theology, and especially practical theology, has related to the social sciences, charismatic spirituality and theories of truth and knowledge. Part Two progresses into six empirical studies on charismatic worship, glossolalia and postmodernity, women and prophetic activity, the 'Toronto Blessing', healing and socialization. Each chapter ends with methodological reflection and suggestions for renewed theological praxis, enforcing the value of such methods of study for an understanding of charismatic Christianity.